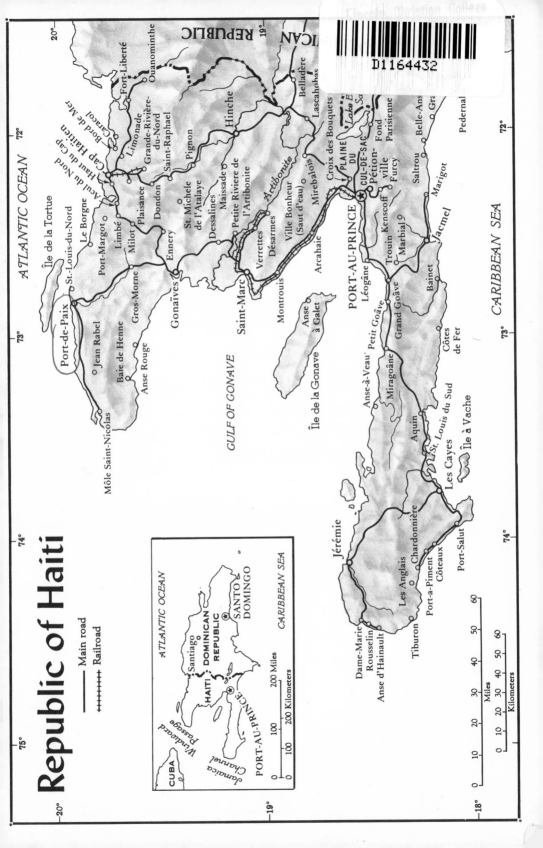

Republic of Haiti

—— Main road
++++++ Railroad

ICR STUDIES:1

General Editor: Theodore L. Stoddard

RELIGION AND POLITICS

IN

HAITI

A Haitian family, by M. Stephane. A contemporary
"primitive" painting from the collection of Harold Courlander.

RELIGION AND POLITICS

IN

HAITI

Two Essays by Harold Courlander and Rémy Bastien

With a Preface by Richard P. Schaedel

 Published by the Institute for Cross-Cultural Research
4000 Albemarle Street, N.W., Washington, D. C. 20016

Library of Congress Catalog Card Number: 66-26633

Manufactured in the United States of America by
The Goetz Company, Washington, D. C.

This publication should be cited as *Religion and Politics in
Haiti,* ICR Studies 1, Washington, D. C.: Institute for Cross-Cultural
Research, 1966.

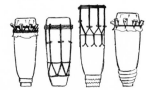

FOREWORD

The number of cross-cultural problems created by the impact of the more-developed nations on the people of the less-developed ones is increasing inevitably and irrevocably. To some extent the effects of this impact can be predicted and controlled if valid information about the problems facing the developing people is made available to researchers, planners, technicians, and travelers. The Institute for Cross-Cultural Research — an independent, nonprofit, educational organization supported at the present time by grants and contributions — intends to serve this expanding audience with intelligibly written, descriptive, and theoretical publications prepared by respected authorities in the behavioral sciences.

In this publication and in others to follow, ICR will try to stimulate better understanding of human problems in the developing world. Such a problem is the relationship between religion and politics — and Haiti offers an outstanding example. ICR is pleased, therefore, to present these contributions by three eminent observers of Haitian life.

ICR is grateful to the United Nations, the Pan American Union, and the National Geographic Society for providing a number of the photographs reproduced in this book.

Many hands have assisted in the production of this volume. Dr. Janice Hopper provided expert editorial guidance from the beginning. Carole DuPré prepared the Supplementary Bibliography and assisted in editorial research. Georgia Rhoades supervised the preparation of all the materials for the printer. Dorothy Conlon, Valerie Auserehl, and Angelika Jackson undertook a variety of necessary tasks which are gratefully acknowledged.

Theodore L. Stoddard
Director
July 1966

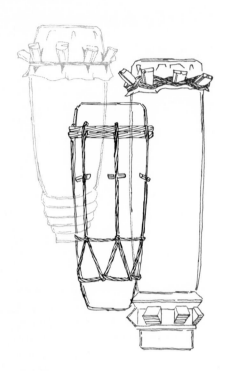

THE AUTHORS

RICHARD P. SCHAEDEL, editor of the recently established *Latin American Research Review,* has been associated with the University of Texas Institute of Latin American Studies since 1964, with faculty status as a Lecturer in Anthropology. A Yale Ph.D. (1951), Schaedel has had a variety of archaeological, human resources, and community development research and teaching experience in Latin America. As a community analyst for the United States Agency for International Development he served in Haiti from 1959 through 1962; he has since worked for the agency in Nicaragua and Venezuela. Schaedel also has taught and studied in Peru, in Chile, and in Argentina. His early work in Peru was as a Wenner-Gren fellow.

Among Schaedel's published work are the following: "Major Ceremonial and Population Centers in Northern Peru," in the *Proceedings* of the Twenty-Ninth Congress of Americanists, 1951; "Los recursos humanos del Departamento de Puno," in *Southern Peru Regional Development Plan,* 1960; and "Land Reform Studies," a summary article in the *Latin American Research Review,* Volume I, No. I, Fall 1965. His findings as a community analyst in Haiti have been distributed by the Agency for International Development in mimeographed form under the title *An Essay on the Human Resources of Haiti* (1962).

HAROLD COURLANDER is a political commentator for the Voice of America. Before coming to the United States Information Agency in 1960, he had been press officer for the United Nations and for the United States Mission to the United Nations. During World War II, he was chief of news and features operations for the Office of War Information in India. He also spent two years in Eritrea and Ethiopia. His scholarship, talents, and interests are reflected in a variety of art forms; he has written two novels and a play, and collected several volumes of folklore and folk music. Part of his folk music collection has been released on records of the Ethnic Folkways Library, of which Courlander was for ten years General Editor. His work has been supported by two Guggenheim fellowships and a Wenner-Gren Foundation grant. He made many trips to Haiti between 1932 and 1957. Appropriately, his first published work was *Haiti Singing.*

Courlander's study of Haitian life and lore, *The Drum and the Hoe,* is regarded by fellow scholars as a definitive work. His Negro folkplay,

Swamp Mud, written during his University of Michigan days, won the first Avery Hopward award in 1931. His early novel, *The Caballero,* depicted Dominican life under dictator Rafael Trujillo; more recently he has written a fictional account of Negro life in the American South, *The Big Old World of Richard Creeks.* His folklore collections include African tales, tales of Asia and the Far East under the title *The Tiger's Whisker,* Indonesian tales, and *Terrapin's Pot of Sense* dealing with the southern United States.

RÉMY BASTIEN is Chief of Studies of the Pan American Union Inter-american Housing and Planning Center in Bogotá, Colombia. A native Haitian, Bastien was educated at the Collège Saint Martial of Port-au-Prince. He took his M.A. in Archaeology in 1947 at the Escuela Nacional de An-tropología e Historia in Mexico on a Rockefeller Foundation fellowship, and his Ph.D. *cum laude* at the same institution in 1951, on a Wenner-Gren Foundation grant.

Bastien was named Secretary General of the one-year-old Haitian Bureau of Ethnology in 1942 when Dr. François Duvalier was one of the assistants. After completing his work for the degree of Master of Arts (1944-1947) Bastien returned to Haiti as assistant director of Alfred Métraux's UNESCO pilot project in the valley of Marbial, Haiti. He has served Haiti as a diplomat, scholar, and teacher, and has taught at the university level in Mexico, Haiti, Puerto Rico, and Colombia. He is the author of "Haitian Rural Family Organization," in Mintz, S. and W. Davenport, Eds., *Working Papers in Caribbean Social Organization,* Social and Economic Studies 10:380-535: Institute of Social and Economic Research, Univ. College of the West Indies, 1961; "The Role of the Intellectual in Haitian Plural Society," in *Social and Cultural Pluralism in the Caribbean,* St. Whitelock, Otto V., Ed., 1960; "El vodu en Haiti," in *Cuadernos Americanos,* 11, 61:1, enero-febrero, 1952, 147-164, and other papers.

CONTENTS

Maps

Illustrations

Frontispiece. A Haitian Family, by M. Stephane. A Contemporary "Primitive" Painting from the Collection of Harold Courlander

FOLLOWING PAGE 26

PREFACE

by Richard P. Schaedel

The editors of this series have seen fit to combine two topics which would seem to be almost incongruous in most modern societies, namely how folk religion influences and is influenced by the body politic. Yet in Haiti many things are incongruous. When analyzed in terms of the criteria of economic development, as compared with the rest of Latin America, Haiti usually stands at the bottom. A recent quantification of 24 criteria associated with socio-economic development in Latin America countries showed that on a scale of 1-10 (highest to lowest) Haiti placed 10th on all counts ranging from per capita income to illiteracy. A parade of economic advisers from the United States and the principal international agencies and banks, who have analyzed the Haitian economy over the past decade, have sounded a dismally uniform note of despair in formulating their pessimistic forecasts for development planning. Political analysts and public administration experts have been equally perplexed by the Haitian polity in trying to devise a rational or at least feasible program of institutional reform.

In these two papers we have an imaginative approach to understanding the complexity of Haitian culture and polity. Two writers from entirely distinct backgrounds and with clearly different socio-political orientations attempt to show how Vodoun has been, since before the birth of the Haitian nation, inextricably associated with the adventures of the state and underline the significant role which it is playing in the current episode.

These introductory remarks are offered to provide a kind of broad context wherein certain special features of the Haitian scene are underscored which will help the reader to understand and evaluate the expositions of Courlander and Bastien.

In the sense of a traditional as contrasted with a transitional society, perhaps Haiti comes closest in the Western Hemisphere to being traditional. Despite a constitutional government system in operation since 1806, it has never really made up its mind that it is not an absolute monarchy. The last emperor was Soulouque (1847-1859), but Duvalier appears on the threshhold of assuming the imperial toga as the logical next step to his having been elected perpetual president.

It is not hard to see why the president wields such absolute power when one considers that 92% of the population lives in hamlets of less than 2,500 people under military government. The remaining 8% — from teachers to managers of public enterprise — are largely dependent upon state appointments for their jobs. The president protects his prerogative to hire and fire anyone in the entire federal system as jealously as he guards the tradition of not fiscalizing income from public enterprise. An encroachment on these rights is considered a violation of sovereignty. This is the prime reason for the recent disruption of relations between Haiti and international — including the United States—Technical Assistance Programs. The narrow sphere of jobs in private enterprise, administered by the mulatto elite and a small Lebanese colony, is the only one not controlled by the executive.

While a capitalist economy has existed in Haiti from the time of the French Colonialism, entrepreneurship on the grand scale has been a monopoly of the mulatto elite, reinforced by a few foreign businessmen. It is a striking commentary on the Black Haitian value system that, despite the extremely acute manipulations of the low-status *marchande* (itinerant market woman) which demonstrate the extraordinary capabilities of the Haitian female for participating in the capitalist economy, mercantilism does not enjoy a very high status. The successful petty entrepreneur does not parlay her winnings into big business, but prefers to invest them in educating the children for respectable professions and real estate. Something of the medieval taint is ascribed to the practice of commerce.

When the government engages in business, however, as it does in sugar, cacao, and tobacco, the managers and administrative personnel are considered to have high status *qua* civil servants.

It is often said with pride that Haiti is a peasant country. This is true in contrast to most of Latin America which is beset by extreme maldistribution of cultivable lands, but the peasant society is far from idyllic. The *Code Rural* governing the rural area dates from 1845 and the only civic right extended to the rural inhabitant since then is to vote for president. The feared *Chef de section* is the rural appointive representative who may hold sway over as many as 20,000 souls and occasionally emulates a rustic satrapy based upon a hierarchy of unsalaried aides and a dispersed harem. Permission to exercise all elementary rights including that of assembly must be channeled through this official. Such petitions usually involve "fees" and are resorted to only under duress.

Taxing procedures are handled by a ubiquitous office, euphemistically named Bureau des Contributions which assesses either a tax or rent (many peasants are not sure which) on their miniscule estates. A strong pressure is maintained by the urban populations to keep the rural peasantry in their place and illiterate. All export crops the peasant produces are sold obligatorily to state-licensed speculators.

The state, as represented by each incumbent administration, is constantly aware of the necessity to reinforce its position of power and of striking a balance between the rural and urban elements. At the outset of the Duvalier regime, it felt that the urban sectors, influenced in large part by the mulatto elite and defeated candidates, might prove a focus of opposition. To this extent it made a concerted effort to appeal to the peasantry with a platform of long overdue reforms which included local civil government, literacy programs, and community development assistance. In so doing it threatened to pit the suppressed peasantry against the urban populace.

It soon realized that such reforms would represent the delegation of too much power to the rural populace and retrenched its position, preferring to use the bread and circus formula of bringing large masses of peasants to the capital for the two or three day celebrations marking milestones in the Duvalier rise to power.

Despite these drastic reversals of state policy the experience of organizing local self-help councils and the dissemination of reading materials and ideas about community improvement from vaccinations to feeder roads has produced an impact in the rural areas the consequences of which are still not clear.

The Haitian peasant has been traditionally accustomed to looking after his own welfare and security. However much he respects the power of the state, he distrusts it. Almost imperceptibly, the peasant has been adjusting to a changing environment. Without outside prodding he has given indications that attitudes toward large families are changing. Polygamy, which was eminently feasible in the nineteenth century with much land and few men, is decreasing in the densely populated rural areas. By patronizing almost exclusively the network of country markets the peasant has successfully challenged the hegemony of the urban merchants who exercise taxing and pricing prerogatives in the towns. In depressed areas, he has shown ingenuity in developing supplementary sources of income through artisanry and migratory labor.

In short, the peasantry is resourceful and is not lacking in aspirations, but it is realistic about their realization. The successful farmer tries to send his children to be educated in the city and to learn a trade. He will be anxious to try new crops and techniques, but not at the expense of risking his security investment in the old standbys. He is conscious of the institutional barriers to his advancement and prefers circumventing them rather than pressing for their elimination.

Despite the apparent accumulation of frustrations that characterize Haitian peasant existence, he is characterized by outsiders as basically a "happy" type. However inappropriate this term, most observers agree that the Haitian peasant possesses a high degree of equanimity, not infrequently accompanied by a great sense of dignity and a pervasive sense of humor. This poise stems in large part from the inheritance of a rich oral tradition which the original Haitians brought from Africa as slaves, and later elaborated upon mostly in the form of proverbs, in improvised songs, and in stories, fables, and legends. The Creole language lends itself most appropriately to these pithy, epigrammatic expressions of an eclectic but nonetheless profound philosophy of life. Vodoun provides it a sort of theological base.

Reading the proverbs reveals a world in which the powerful triumph and the weak are destroyed, but in which the vain are often tricked and the hypocritical punished. Animals seem to serve as personality types that are either ridiculed or praised. One is constantly warned against believing that things are as they appear. There is no place in Haitian maxims for "seeing is believing," but "all that glitters is not gold" would do admirably. The transitory quality of power is frequently remarked upon. As in nature so with human beings, one must be careful of traps, camouflage, and apparent bountifulness. The path of least resistance seldom turns out to be the best. From this emerges the philosophy of a *Bon Dieu* (God) who presides over the universe, who is neither kindly nor particularly vengeful, and with whom one must come to terms.

In view of *Bondieu's* lack of intervention in affairs of this world, the role of operations is ascribed to the Vodoun pantheon and the lesser household deities. Their behavior and the more routine ways of placating them are generally known by most Haitians. But when problems arise, usually sickness, the *houngans* are called upon to determine which of the deities has been offended and what specific remedial measures are necessary. The knowledge of the *houngan* and *mambo,* derived from visions and dreams, has qualified them for entering into direct contact and mediation with the deities.

Some writers have called attention to the prevalence of disease in Haiti and the concomitant anxiety as providing the ideal climate for Vodoun to flourish. So as to appear ultimately more effective, the *houngan* has been accused of preying on this anxiety and even of prolonging an illness. But the therapeutic effect and recreative quality of Vodoun are equally important in providing emotional enrichment and relaxation to the rural Haitian. The nonsacred *bamboche* is the normal outlet for the family or group celebration, whether the occasion be a birthday, wedding, or other occasion. It has been patterned after Vodoun assemblies, but without the presence of officiating priest, attendants, or *hounfor*. The annual *Ra-ra* dance groups which perform during Lent are also basically recreative and provide an outlet for group participation. This is the preferred occasion for sexual license.

It would appear, as our authors indicate, that Vodoun and its associated patterns provide the core of a number of institutions that are lacking in the formal structure of Haitian society and without which rural life would be extremely drab. Catholicism, if only for the lack of clergy, could not penetrate into the rural community, but more important its spiritual content appears to be too removed from the use of earthy symbols and the blending of nature and human experience which are cornerstones of the Haitian world view. Protestantism has moved into the countryside and gained converts because it supplies active group participation in singing congregations and concerns itself with practical matters such as healing, low cost baptisms and marriages, and rudimentary education. Its intransigence to Vodoun, however, has made reconversion almost as frequent. Formal religion then has not made much headway in Haiti. One might say that it has the same distribution as enfranchised private enterprise. Both are largely limited to the towns and the capital and are primarily important to the mulatto elite.

Vodoun has another advantage over formal religions. In addition to being functionally effective at the village level, it does not challenge the sovereignty of the state as do Catholicism and the more established Protestant faiths.

In a despotic state organization, an autonomous church is bound to chart a hazardous course; and this has been the fate of the Catholic clergy in Haiti. Even where the church has been obliged to make generous concessions to the state, and to operate under strict overt and covert state surveillance, its authority over its own church personnel is constantly challenged by the state and its role has been drastically curtailed by Duvalier to the point where it provides a hollow echo for state ceremonialism.

Small wonder then that Vodoun has moved in to fill the void. Formerly obliged to operate under a certain discreet cover, the *houngans* may now seek public recognition with prestigious state patrons. High government officials make gaudy displays of sponsoring special Vodoun ceremonies. Whether their faith in Vodoun is sincere is an academic question. It is clear that many pay lip service to the cult for the obvious gain in popular support that results. Bastien is doubtless correct in referring to Duvalier's adherence to Vodoun as basically political, although we detect a real ambivalence in the attitude of most Haitians (even before Duvalier) who in moments of crisis or acute anxiety are wont to resort to Vodoun.

Vodoun like Creole quite clearly embodies a core of deeply rooted Africanist beliefs and modes of cognition which are the essence of the Haitian national personality. However much superstition and fetishes may reflect the superficial trappings of primitive cultism, there is a deeper spiritual content in Vodoun that has been reinforced by its long history and its traditional role of protector to the community and family that no amount of "enlightenment" is likely to eradicate. One of the purposes of these two essays is to focus on the question of the apparent growth or renascence of Vodoun in recent years in Haiti. The points made by the authors are cogent and debatable. On many aspects they disagree, yet they both affirm that economic and social progress in Haiti signifies the extinction of Vodoun.

Unfortunately the analyses and interpretations of Vodoun made by Bastien and Courlander rest on fragmentary data. Despite the overwhelming importance of Vodoun and a copious but unreliable literature, it has received minimal scientific study by scholars. The more detailed accounts by Rigaud and Métraux are based upon a few informants. Most anthropologists have difficulty obtaining information on Vodoun and are obliged to concentrate on other aspects of Haitian culture, leading to the unfortunate impression that Vodoun is really not too significant in the total pattern.

The pharmacopoeia available to an able *houngan* is formidable and a great part of it is unknown to western medicine. His reliance on and skillful utilization of this basic knowledge of herbs, both remedial and harmful, combined with psychotherapeutical techniques in consultation and treatment are his principal means for establishing a powerful hold on the community in which he practices. They lie at the core of the attraction and power of Vodoun. We know precious little about the ethnobotany of Haiti, and it is probably one of the richest in the hemisphere. *Houngans* cannot rest their fame upon a diploma or the possession of a *hounfor*. They have to produce to stay in business; and the fact that they proliferate indicates that their stock-in-trade is usually effective. Until we know how they operate in a very precise way, we cannot really measure their effectiveness either for good or for evil.

One of the outstanding characteristics of Vodoun that emerges from a reading of these two essays is its tremendous flexibility and adaptability to changing conditions. Despite the lack of an organized priesthood, and despite the allegations of regional cults (no one has actually researched this), the corpus of beliefs and practices appears to retain a remarkable cohesiveness. Several variant African religions have been fused in a new synthesis, new concepts like the Catholic Sainthood are incorporated into the system, and the whole development of Pétro rites appears to be an independent contribution of nineteenth century *houngans*.

Vodoun appears likely to continue as a repository for the ethos of Haitian culture. We predict that Vodoun will modify itself as insular Haiti confronts the universe of modernism around it. In this ecumenical world, even a new kind of syncretism between Protestantism and Vodoun is not unthinkable. Just as the enigmatic character of Haiti's first 165 years has puzzled historians, and as the analysis of the contemporary scene has confounded Western economists and political specialists alike, so the forecast of future trends is likely to prove even more evasive and exasperating. Courlander and Bastien provide a refreshingly original focus for perceiving key relationships in the present Haitian dilemma. This represents a trend which must be encouraged if we are one day to arrive at a degree of comprehension, permitting us to interact on a plane of international harmony with the world's first Negro Republic and the second nation to achieve independence in the Western Hemisphere.

VODOUN IN HAITIAN CULTURE

by Harold Courlander

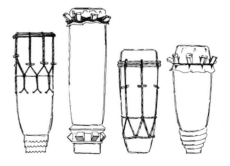

VODOUN IN HAITIAN CULTURE[1]

by Harold Courlander

1 THE LAND AND ITS PEOPLE

The Island of Hispaniola,[2] lying on the northern rim of the Caribbean, was one of the first lands of the Western Hemisphere affected by the European exploration and expansion in the late fifteenth century. Columbus sighted the island in December of 1492. While his ships were sailing along the northern coast, his flagship, the *Santa Maria,* ran aground at a place believed to be a few miles east of the present city of Cap Haïtien. The vessel was dismantled, and from its timbers and hardware a temporary settlement was built. Forty men were left there to await Columbus' return from Spain, but by the time Columbus touched again at the site on his second voyage, the garrison had vanished, presumably killed off by Indians. Another settlement was established, and within a relatively few years the entire Caribbean area was the scene of vigorous exploration and claims by Spain, France, and England.

The Indians who inhabited Hispaniola (or Haiti, the indigenous name, meaning Mountainous Land) when the Spanish arrived were mainly Arawaks or Tainos, an agricultural people who had migrated into the Caribbean from the South American mainland. The Spanish settlers sought, above all other objectives, to make their fortunes by finding gold. They confiscated the gold trinkets worn by the peaceful Arawaks and pressed the entire population into service in a frenetic search for the yellow metal. Every adult Arawak (beginning at the age of fourteen) was required to furnish a stipulated amount of gold four times a year. The Arawaks were also put to forced labor in agriculture, and some were shipped to Spain as slaves. The mortality among the Indians was high. Many of them fled to the mountains or took to the sea to find refuge on other islands, and it was said that thousands of Arawaks poisoned themselves in desperation. Within fifteen years about four-fifths or more of the original Arawak population had disappeared. It was at this point that the Spanish settlers and fortune hunters began to look elsewhere for labor, and thus began the importation of slaves from Africa.

African slave cargoes began to arrive in Hispaniola about 1510 or 1512. These Africans and others that followed during the next three centuries were the ethnic strains from which most contemporary Haitians are descended. Old records show that among the slaves brought to what is now Haiti were Foulas, Poulards, Sosos, Bambarras, Kiambaras, Mandingos, and Wolofs from northwest Africa; Aradas (Fons), Mahis, Hausas, Ibos, Anagos (Yorubas), Bini, Takwas, Fidas, Amines, Fanti, Agouas, Sobos, Limbas, and Adjas from the coast and interior of the great bulge of Africa; Salongos, Mayombés, Mousombés, Moundongues, Bumbas, Kangas, and others from the Congo basin. The slave trade was indiscriminate, getting its cargoes wherever it could, without concern as to whether the slaves were tillers of the field, craftsmen, or members of princely families. So among those Africans brought to Haiti were people from all stations of life and from a wide stretch of the African continent. They brought with them tribal traditions, social values, unwritten literature, systems of worship, and a particularized African attitude toward nature and the supernatural.

Though there is implicit evidence that competent craftsmen were among the transplanted Africans, the ancient crafts withered in the New World setting. For this, the slave system itself was largely responsible. Such woodcarvers as there may have been found no wealthy or princely patrons to encourage them to make stools, ancestor images, fertility figures, and other objects. Nor did they have much time or energy for such things. Furthermore, the disruption of cult and family life diminished the need for elaborate ritual objects. When such objects were required, inferior makeshifts were accepted. Traditional West African ironwork also disappeared for much the same reasons. Those who worked at the forge worked under the supervision of the masters, and they used their craft for making prosaic plantation objects such as hoes and other tools, or hardware to grace the colonial mansions. Of the ancient brasscasting art of Nigeria, no trace at all was left. Nevertheless, here and there an isolated ironworker must have kept something of the old forging tradition alive, for iron ritual objects have been found which are stylistically related to objects known in Dahomey, Nigeria, and other parts of West Africa. So, too, a few old woodcarvings reminiscent of true African style have survived, and many of the cult drums still seen today are in pure African tradition.

It was the nonmaterial African inheritance that survived most vigorously in Haiti. Stories and legends, religious concepts, herb and leaf doctoring, the belief in and practice of magic, music, dance, manners, concepts of right and wrong, attitudes toward marriage, attitudes toward the dead—

these elements of African life persisted strongly. The most dynamic of the survivals was Vodoun, as we shall see later.

In their impatience to find fabulous treasure, the Spanish paid little attention to agriculture, and they increasingly neglected the western end of the island, what is now the Republic of Haiti. French settlers moved into the western region and plantations began to spring up in the alluvial plains. In 1697, the western end of the island was ceded to France, and it was known thereafter, until the Haitian Revolution, as Saint-Domingue. Under French administration the colony flourished and became one of the great colonial prizes in the New World. It was during the period of French control that the Haitian cultural amalgam was achieved. French ways of doing things and seeing things were blended with the African inheritance. These blending processes sometimes produced unique results. The slaves took over the French vocabulary of the masters and unconsciously transformed it into a new language, Creole, which is spoken today not only in Haiti but in other parts of the West Indies where the French colonized — Martinique, Guadaloupe, and Carriacou, for example. It is spoken also in Trinidad, which took in Haitian sugar planters and their slaves at the time the Haitian Revolution was brewing; it was also spoken in Louisiana when that region of the North American mainland was under French control. The Creole language, while based on French vocabulary, uses grammatical patterns and verb conjugations which seem to relate to West African speech. The French words themselves are agglutinated or truncated to accommodate to more familiar rhythmic patterns. The development of this language among the slaves undoubtedly played a part in the Haitians' growing awareness of themselves as a single people.

By the time the Haitian Revolution came at the end of the eighteenth century, Haitian culture was composed of elements of both French and African traditions mixed together in varied proportions. Some Haitians, indeed, were as French as the Frenchmen whom the Revolution evicted from the country. A special class of *affranchi* had appeared on the scene, primarily mulattos who had gained their liberty. Under French rule, the *affranchis* had developed large economic interests. Under the *Code Noir* of 1687, they were French citizens, with all citizens' rights including the right to own slaves. While such rights as they were legally endowed with were increasingly infringed and eroded during the eighteenth century, many of the *affranchis* continued to regard themselves as Frenchmen. Indeed, even some of the leaders of the Haitian Revolution seemed more French than Haitian.

Thus Haiti was in some respects African, in some respects European, and in some respects a blend. Out of this situation at the time of the Revolution there emerged an internal political and psychological conflict that has persisted to this day — the conflict between Blacks and mulattos. The mulattos seemed to the Blacks to be related to the former white colonists. Though the mulattos had been abused by the whites, nevertheless they had been a class apart with a status far more desirable than that of the slaves. They had prospered, and many of them had themselves owned slaves and plantations. Many were educated. They spoke French rather than the *sauvage* language of the countryside. They regarded their darker brothers as peasants or country bumpkins, while the Blacks, for their part, regarded the elite mulattos as effete, given to grand manners, and the possessors of a special status to which they were not entitled. After all, it was the Blacks under L'Ouverture, Dessalines, and Christophe who had secured the liberty of the nation. But this malaise was compounded by the split between the north and the south at the time of Christophe's ascendancy to power in Cap Haïtien. The south, under the leadership of the mulatto Alexandre Pétion, broke away. The support for Pétion's rule came from the mulatto class, though Pétion himself was permissive and democratic in his attitudes and manifested no color prejudice of his own. His successor in 1818 was Jean-Pierre Boyer, another mulatto. Two years later Christophe died, and the country was reunited under Boyer. Thereafter, Haiti was ruled from Port-au-Prince by a mulatto class. Boyer was ousted by a revolution in 1843. Those who seized power briefly were also largely mulatto, and they undertook to eliminate all Negro influence from government. Another revolution came the following year, one of its announced purposes being to put a dark president into the Palace. The mulatto monopoly was broken, and Haiti's presidents for some years to come were Negro. But the sense of confrontation has persisted, explicit or unstated, to the present day. Though the elite group, in which mulattos are a major element, constitutes perhaps five percent of the population, it has had an influence far in excess of its numbers.

Haiti is a unique country in the Caribbean, and probably what made it so, more than any other single factor, was the timing of its revolution. Cuba's freedom did not come until the end of the nineteenth century; Jamaica's and Trinidad's not until the middle of the twentieth century. During all their years as colonies they continued — for better or worse, according to the individual case — to have close relations with the nations that ruled them. There was a long period during which European cultural and political influence was exerted. This sustained relationship between the colonizer and the colonized has unquestionably affected the outlook of Jamaicans, Trinidadians, and others whose complete independence has only recently been achieved. In anthropological terms, there has been a long-sustained acculturation process at work. Beyond that, there has been a continued infusion of new ideas and dynamics. But Haiti's political and social ties with Europe were weakened when it accomplished its revolution more than a century and a half ago. To a great extent the nation as a whole became isolated culturally from the rest of the world. Except for the intellectual contacts the elite had with Europe and North America, and the commercial contacts necessary for the disposal of its sugar, sisal, bananas, dyewood, mahogany, coffee, and other crops, Haiti had little communication with other nations. It had, in fact, little in common with them. For most of the world it was a curious, exotic, and largely unknown place. Technological developments were slow to reach Haiti; and having reached Haiti they were regarded there as largely irrelevant to Haitian life. In fact, even some of the rudimentary technology of a century or more ago remains irrelevant. Draft animals and plows, for example, are useless on the steep mountain slopes and in the tiny garden patches. And even if useful, draft animals could not be properly fed and cared for on many of the limited landholdings. The peasant plots have become smaller rather than larger through the years, mainly through the division of land among heirs, and the machete and the hoe remain the basic tools for most of the rural population.

It is not only in technology and material culture that Haiti has been isolated, but in nonmaterial culture as well. Old traditions, some useful and worthy, others harmful and corrosive, continue on. Because the arts and techniques of modern society are not available or not pertinent, Haitians stand by such of the ancient arts and techniques as they still retain. Africanisms persist more strongly in Haiti than in any part of the New World save perhaps among the so-called Bush Negroes of the Guianas. In some ways Haiti is not greatly different from what it was a centruy ago. For anthropologists and folklorists, therefore, it is a source of fascination. There is no other island in the Caribbean that has such rich survivals of African-style music and dancing, and of religious beliefs and practices that relate to ancient African tradition. The early independence of the country and the subsequent poverty of opportunity together have made modern Haiti what it is.

Perhaps the strongest "outside" influence in Haiti over the years has been the Catholic Church. Although the Church has helped educate a goodly portion of those who have been educated, it has not offered anything to substitute for older traditions. The consequence is that most of those who proclaim adherence to the Catholic faith also adhere to Vodoun. And the Catholic influence, like Vodoun itself, has been a conservative force in Haitian life.

By and large, the Catholic Church, unlike some of the Protestant denominations, has tended to be tolerant and permissive about Vodoun.[3] But there have been times when the Church has brought heavy pressures on the Government to outlaw and disband the cults. These pressures have been both intolerant and ill-advised. Well publicized Church campaigns against the practice of Vodoun were conducted in 1896, 1913, and 1939. Again in the early 1940's there was a concerted campaign. This time the ritual paraphernalia of a large number of cults were confiscated, cult centers destroyed, and cult leaders subjected to intimidation and ridicule, and at least temporarily driven from their communities. Undoubtedly, there have been numerous local incidents of this kind through the years. At various times government officials have acquiesced to pressures from the Church to "do something" about Vodoun. Often they have resisted, if not out of personal identification with Vodoun, at least out of political considerations or out of plain common sense. For Vodoun is too fundamental a part of Haitian life, not only in the cult temple, but in all aspects of daily living.

Haitians have suffered economically and socially for a very long time, and the suffering continues. The country has a rocky, mountainous terrain with relatively small amounts of fertile, tillable land. The soil is overworked and eroded. The best land in the large valleys is owned by large corporations. The country is overpopulated—the most densely populated nation in the Western Hemisphere. Peasant landholdings are shrinking in size. There is little literacy, and health services and nutrition are grossly inadequate. The gap between the wealthy and the population at large is widening. There is a malformed and underdeveloped political consciousness. Among the elite there is little feeling of social responsibility for the rural masses. Government frequently has been ineffective and often unscrupulous. And today, after years of a slow but steady decline, the economic situation is probably worse than at any time in Haitian history.

Nevertheless, the Haitian goes about his tasks as though poverty were an old friend. The largest part of Haitian productive life is agrarian. Small peasant landholdings fill the valley pockets not suitable for plantations and cover the rocky mountainsides up to the cloud level. Some of the "gardens," as they are called, are on steep slopes that have been eroding for generations. Vast stands of timber have been cut off the land for construction, household fuel, and lime kilns, speeding up the process of erosion. This is the heritage of today's peasant farmer. An estimated three and a half to four million Haitians must be fed off this land. More than three hundred persons must share each square mile of soil. But most of the land surface of Haiti is formidable to farming. Two-thirds of the land area is untillable by modern standards. There is less than one acre of useful land per person, and the best of it is farmed by sugar and sisal corporations.

Typical gardens grow such crops as maize, millet, coffee, bananas, plantains, beans, yams, sweet potatoes, and manioc. Citrus, mango, and avocado trees seem to grow at random. In the delta regions rice is grown. Along the coast are numerous villages in which fishing is the main occupation. Contrary to the age old stereotype of tropical life, most Haitians have to work hard, and this is particularly true of farmers. Their tools are rudimentary. Machetes are used for a wide variety of purposes—cane cutting, making mortars, butchering meat, clearing brush, and felling trees. Hoes are used to turn over the earth before planting and for tilling afterwards. For most *habitants* (peasant farmers) there do not exist such implements as plows, wagons, or wheelbarrows. Crops and garden produce to be sold are carried to market on the head or by donkey back, and sometimes the round trip distance is as much as thirty or forty miles. Some habitations have water nearby, but country people frequently have to fetch their water from rivers or springs a half mile away. Corn and millet meal are not bought at the store, but are pulverized at home in a mortar. Most country people build their own houses, and many dig their own lime and process it themselves to plaster the outside walls of their houses. The amount of work required to produce a minimal living is considerable. There is, of course, a never-ending commerce in foodstuffs and other necessities, but in effect this is largely trade-in-kind. A woman who takes produce to market may receive cash if she sells it, but she spends part or all of her cash on things her household needs, so that she may return home with a few pennies or none at all. Often direct barter is resorted to. As far as most country people are concerned, it is essentially a barter economy. The per capita income fifteen years ago was estimated to be between twenty-five and thirty-five dollars a year. It is probably even less today.

The division of labor between men and women follows a traditional pattern. It is the women who are seen in great numbers on the roads and trails on market days, but behind these marketing activities lies the work of the men. It is the men who clear and break the ground, plant, cultivate, and harvest the crops. They cut the timber, build the houses, dig and process the lime, cut and transport wood for fuel, make charcoal, and build terraces for the mountainside gardens. In the coastal villages it is the men who go to sea to fish. Those who work for wages cut cane and sisal, load ships, build roads, and perform other heavy labor. The women run the household, care for the young children, carry water, launder, cook, sew, play a supporting role in the fields, and transport garden produce, charcoal, or other commodities to the market. Frequently the woman is business manager for the household. Occasionally she can put away small savings of her own from the proceeds of special projects. Children slip into supporting roles at an early age, doing any routine workaday tasks within their competence.

Deep-rooted in Haitian tradition is the concept of communal effort in the fields. The exchange of labor is formalized in the institution of the *coumbite*. The word probably derives from the Spanish *convite*, meaning "invitation," but the institution is an old one common to many West African peoples. Among the Fon it is called *dokpwe*, among the Kpelle *ku*, and among the Mambila *kurum*. The Haitian *coumbite* may be a permanent type of organization with a fixed membership, or a makeshift arrangement for a particular situation. A member of the group holds a *coumbite* by notifying his fellow members that on a certain day his fields will need clearing or tilling. When the men (or, in come cases, women) gather, they work to the accompaniment of music played on drums, bamboo trumpets, or conch horns. A small group of six or seven may work as a single unit, usually advancing abreast across the field. If the *coumbite* is a large one, the men may divide into two groups which work in competition with one another. Part and parcel of the *coumbite* is the social evening that follows. When the work is done, the men go to the house of the host, where a special meal has been prepared for them. This may be followed by a social dance. Another day, the *coumbite* works on the land of another member. Every man in the organization has his fields worked in turn, or whenever he needs help.

For recreation, the Haitian has his social dancing, cock fights, gambling games such as *mayamba* and *wari*, cards, and cheap drinks, carbonated or alcoholic. There is much socializing, though, in various activities that are not essentially recreational. The *coumbite* is one such social opportunity, as are wakes for the dead. Even the rituals of the Vodoun cult have considerable social incentive. Hard pressed as he is, the Haitian has not forgotten how to laugh and enjoy himself with the opportunities his setting makes available.

AFRICAN RELIGIOUS SURVIVALS
IN THE NEW WORLD

Haiti is not the only New World setting in which African religious activity survived after the slave trade came to an end. In Venezuela, Brazil, the Guianas, Cuba, and various other Caribbean regions there are communities and cult centers where African religions persist. In still other Afro-American communities there are recognizable vestiges of African religious patterns. African rites of various tribes were held in Louisiana during slavery days and for some time thereafter. Fragmentary aspects of African religious tradition were observed and documented in the Georgia Sea Islands, and are known to have survived there into the twentieth century. In various instances, survivals in some New World communities became submerged under or absorbed into essentially Christian religious institutions.

Whereas single, unrelated elements of African tradition often disappeared and were forgotten, there were certain constellations of closely related ideas that reinforced and helped to preserve each other. African religious concepts involved music (with emphasis on percussion and rhythm), dance, invocation and placation, water rites, hosts of spirits or demigods, the dead and their relationship with the living, burial rites and imperatives, and to some extent magic. The complex interrelation of these and other elements, in combination with the fact that the religious institution did not depend on survival of material culture, tended to prolong the life of African religious belief and practice.

Cuba is one of those places where African cults continued on strongly into the twentieth century, despite discouragements, obstacles, and harassments periodically imposed on them. From time to time the cults were "exposed" as centers of criminal activities, ritual murders, and "black masses." But there were internal dynamics in African cult life that persecution did not succeed in weakening. The Cuban cults, furthermore, particularly those of Yoruba origin, evolved a unified organization that bound them together and gave them a political weight; this fact alone helped to preserve them and even give them status.

The main Afro-Cuban cult is Yoruban, and is called Lucumí. It retains a pantheon of Yoruban deities or *orisha* that would be called "correct" by modern day African Yorubans. Among them are Légua or Étcho, guardian of the gateway, the highway, and the crossroads; Ogún, patron of iron and iron workers; Otchósi, the hunter; Shango, god of thunder and lightning; Obatalá, god of war and patron of warriors; Panchágara, the river deity; Yemayá or Yalóde, god of the sea; Oko, god of agriculture; and many others that come directly out of Yoruban tradition. The cult priest is called by his Yoruba name; *babalao,* and the paraphernalia of the cult center and religious ritual are traditional. Until at least a few years ago, members of the Lucumí community had preserved elements of the Yoruban language, and frequently spoke to one another in Yoruban.

Another cult which persisted and maintained a separate life for itself was the Arará (known in Haiti as Arada or Rada), Dahomean in origin. It has a pantheon of Dahomean deities that include Damballa, Ayida (the serpent-rainbow god who supports the world on his body); Sogbo; Ogún; Nananbuluku; Hevioso; and many others known to the Vodoun worshippers in Haiti. This cult was for many years strongest in the eastern part of Cuba because of the large number of Haitians who came there from their own island in pursuit of work in the sugar fields.

Separate Congo cults, such as the Kimbísa (also called Mayombé) also were in existence until very recent years, and probably are still active today. There is also a ritualistic fraternal society, the Abakwá, in which traditions of the Calabar Coast (predominantly Ibo) are preserved.

An illicit slave trade continued to bring Africans into Cuba until almost the end of the nineteenth century. As late as the 1940's it was still possible to encounter people in central Cuba who had been born on the African continent. The importation of slaves into Cuba thus went on for a full century after slavery had come to an end in neighboring Haiti. This constant cultural renewal undoubtedly contributed to the preservation of African religious tradition in Cuba, and to the ability of Afro-Cubans to maintain separate and distinct cults, unlike the situation in Haiti where the cults have had a tendency to combine and merge.

African religious tradition also remains alive in Trinidad, one of the southernmost Caribbean islands. Yoruba rites, called Shango (after the Yoru-

ban deity of thunder), have been infiltrated by Christian concepts and by
local invention, but they retain many of the basic elements of the African
prototype. The familiar deities are worshipped—Oshun, Oya, Shakpana,
Ogún, Osain, Beji (Ibeji, Yoruban deity of twins), Eshu (in Cuba, Étcho),
Obatalá, Shango, and others. Some of the names among the Shango deities,
or "powers," as they are called, are not recognizably African; they may be
of local origin or corruptions of African names. As in other locales where
Christian and African influences have blended, each of the deities has a
Christian name. Obatalá, for example, is also called St. Benedict; Oshun,
St. Anne; Shango, St. John; and Eshu (equivalent to Legba in Haiti and Dahomey) is called Satan. Shango cult leaders are called *amombos* (a term
that is also used in Haiti only to designate female cult leaders). There is evidence that Trinidadian Shango traces its antecedents to West Africa only
indirectly. The Afro-American population of the island in the nineteenth
century was largely made up of West Indians brought from other parts of the
Caribbean. Numerous Haitians, for example, were brought to Trinidad when
planters left Haiti at the time of that country's revolution. Many of the terms
used in Shango cult activities are of Haitian, or at least of Creole, derivation.

   The Afro-American community in Brazil has Shango rites which in
some respects are closer to those of the African Yoruba. African traits exist
in attenuated and disguised form in Jamaica in the Cumina cult and among
the Revivalist groups. Among the so-called Bush Negroes of Surinam and
Guyana, African religious tradition is largely that of the Ashanti people.

 VODOUN: ITS ORIGINS AND MEANINGS

   Although slaves brought to Haiti in the sixteenth, seventeenth, and
eighteenth centuries came from a wide stretch of the African continent and
even included people from Central and East Africa, the predominant ethnic
elements were from Dahomey, Nigeria, Togo, and the Congo Basin. The Fon
people of Dahomey (who in Haiti called themselves Arada, after the Dahomean city of Allada) and the Anago (western Yoruba, from what is today Nigeria and Dahomey) were the major influence in the development of Vodoun.
Though they may have started out with their own separate Arada and Anago

institutions, those institutions were so similar in many respects (there had been close tribal contacts in Africa) that a merging of the rites was accomplished simply. Even so, within the cycle of rites now encompassed by Vodoun, the Arada and the Anago elements are sometimes said to be separate though closely related. Vodoun has also accumulated within its framework some rites and deities from other African peoples.

The word Vodoun is Dahomean. In the Fon language it means "spirit" or "deity," and is precisely equivalent to *orisha* in the Yoruba language. Modern Haitians sometimes use the word Vodoun in this sense, though usually the Afro-Haitian deities are called *loa*, from the Bantu, and occasionally *mystère*, from the French. The term Vodoun is generally used to designate the activities and beliefs of the cults. In its strictest sense it refers to the cults built around the religious concepts of the Anago and the Fon (Arada). In a looser sense it includes the rituals of the Ibo cult and various others that have clustered around the Anago and Fon rites. And in the widest, generic application it includes all Afro-Haitian cults including the Congo and the Pétro, the latter considered to be of Creole origin.

Vodoun means more to the Haitian than temple ritual. It is an integrated system of concepts concerning human activities, the relationship between the natural world and the supernatural, and the ties between the living and the dead. It has its own cause and effect system to explain otherwise unexplainable or unpredictable events. It provides guidelines for social behavior and demands that the gods be responsive. In short, it is a true religion which attempts to tie the unknown to the known and establish order where there might otherwise be chaos. For those who believe in Vodoun, no event or episode is a thing in itself. In birth and death, good fortune and bad, the *loa* are somehow involved. Each of the *loa* has characteristics of his (or her) own. Some have special responsibilities in the fields, some at sea, some on the highway, some for the formation of babies in the womb Vodoun also encompasses ritual magic, though some magical practices are felt to be outside the realm of Vodoun's practices and purposes.

There are those who hold that Vodoun is essentially an affair of the extended family (including the ancestors), and that it has only casual need of the cult priest. Nevertheless, the cult priest, usually known as a *houngan*, also as *capla, papaloi* (from *babalao*), and *bocor* (which normally refers to a sorcerer or practitioner of magic), plays a conspicuous role. He translates concepts into formalized action. He can be, and often is, a teacher, a repository of cult knowledge, and a catalyst. He can give practical meaning to symbols and initiate resolutions to religious or workaday dilemmas. To be and do all these things the *houngan* must have the confidence of his community, be dedicated to his profession, have intimate knowledge of the families and individuals who form his following, and, of course, he must be capable of psychological insights. There are many such *houngans,* just as there are others who use their positions ignorantly or unscrupulously.

The cult center is known as the *hounfor.* It may be no more than a poor shack of the kind most people live in, or it may be relatively spacious, furnished with a richesse of ritual objects, and have one or more outside courts where ceremonies and dancing take place. The cult organization of those who follow strictly in the Arada-Anago tradition has a hierarchy with the *houngan* (*mambo* is a woman) at the top. One step below is the *laplace,* the *houngan's* chief assistant. Further down is the *mambo caille,* who cares for the premises. On the next rung down is the *houngénicon,* topmost of the servitors who has passed certain tests and performed the required services. Then, on the bottom, two classes of ordinary servitors: Those who have passed through a fire ordeal demonstrating that they have the favor and protection of the *loa* are called *hounsi kanzo*—"*hounsi* of the fire pot." The lowest order of servitors are the *hounsi bossale*—"wild" *hounsi* not yet far enough advanced to control the *loa* who enter their bodies during a state of possession. Some Vodoun cults have additional orders of officials and servitors.

Each *hounfor* is independent. There is no supreme individual or group to instruct or give direction to the local cults, no Pope or Dalai Lama. A local cult center flourishes if it has the support and trust of the community, fades away if the *houngan* fails to impress the community as being "strong." Servitors recognize the difference between a *houngan* who has *connaissance* and one who has only deficient understanding of tradition and of the character and whims of the deities who must be dealt with. In the cities new *houngans* may set up cult centers without any particular community sanction and take their chances. In the countryside the *houngans* are generally an integral part of the communities in which they practice. When a *houngan's* apprentice (the *laplace*) "takes the *asson,*" as it is said, and becomes a *houngan* in his own right, he may have to meet tests and qualifications set for him by other practicing *houngans.* Or he may simply and quietly slip into his role in the community, and perhaps become influential as time goes by, or remain a small, unimportant Vodoun priest who is called upon occasionally in time of need. In his own community, that is to say, among his own following, he is paramount in religious matters. There is no one higher up to tell him he has erred in this or that, or to give him codified knowledge. If he needs knowledge—*connaissance*—he must seek it out himself. Yet there are standards of competence which no *houngan* can ignore. They are the standards of the profession and the standards of the community the *houngan* serves.

The activities of the cult center and the cult priest are centered on dealing with the *loa* (invoking, asking help or favors, placating their petulance or anger, feeding them at appropriate times); on coping with evil forces set in motion by *loa* or practitioners of magic; on fertility of the fields and human fertility; on serving the spirit of twins; on retiring *loa* from the heads of deceased persons; on remembering and placating the dead ancestors; and on seeing that the dead are properly sent to their abode "Under the Water." Services and ceremonies are multitudinous and never-ending. Once placated or served, the deities must be placated and served again and again. The dead ancestors must be remembered and dealt with over and over again.

In the Afro-Haitian view, the family includes not only all the living who are descended from common ancestors, but the family dead as well. While some Haitians believe that the dead stay in close proximity to the *loa,* others hold that the dead have no special residing place. Whatever their place of residence, the spirits of the dead must be forever coped with. This concept is widely held in West Africa and among Bantu-speaking peoples. When a person dies, he is believed to have a continuing interest in the affairs and welfare of those left behind. But a dead ancestor retains all the characteristics he had in life. He has a human personality. He may be prone to jealousy, irritable, and cantankerous. His feelings may be easily wounded. And because he is concerned with the family welfare and the behavior of his descendants, he may be critical. So while the dead can confer blessings, great care must be taken that they are not offended. They are frequently spoken to, listened to, and placated in the course of any number of different ceremonies. There is a notable category of the dead which requires special services — the twins of earlier generations. The concept of the special attributes of twins, and the particular necessity of pleasing them (and of supplication of the *loa* of twins) is both Yoruba and Fon in origin. The spirits of dead twins can be especially willful and capricious, and unless properly dealt with they may cause illness and misfortune. At least once each year, on dates fixed by local or family custom, services are held for *marassas,* as twins are called.

Thus the Vodoun magico-religious complex has several varieties of non-human beings that have to be contended with. Apart from the dead, the *loa,* and errant souls that may be sent out by *houngans* or *loa* to do mischief, there is a large number of demons and evil spirits of various kinds. Although the demons and evil spirits are largely outside the realm of Vodoun, properly speaking, they have to be counteracted with the powers inherent in Vodoun. The *houngan* or the *bocor* is called on to provide protective amulets or rituals. In addition to protections against supernatural forces, the cult priest is sometimes called upon for ritualistic protections against human enemies. Some *houngans* or *bocors* are also *divineurs* who, through contact with the *loa,* can answer questions about the future, or the whereabouts of lost objects, or the supernatural causes of certain events.

The various cults encompassed by the term Vodoun in its larger sense are not easy to set down diagrammatically because of different degrees of blending and absorption in different regions of Haiti. Had the old cults or "nations" remained independent of one another, as they probably were in early days, they probably would have included the following: Arada (Dahomey or Fon), Anago (Yoruba), Mahi, Ibo, Kanga, Congo (including Moundongue, Solongo, Bumba, etc., or these elements also might have maintained independence), and Pétro (a cult in the African pattern that appears to have originated in Haiti). In certain parts of Haiti one still finds Ibo, Congo, and Nago cults that have resisted absorption, but this pattern does not hold for most of the country. In general, Congo and Pétro tend to go together. Anago is a nation within a nation in the Dahomey rites. The Ibo group is frequently found closely allied with the Arada, though in some cases it has an affinity with the Congo cult.

The *loa* of the Arada-Anago cult are numbered in the hundreds.[4] The principal ones, however, are derived from Fon and Yoruba tradition. Among the traditional Fon deities are the following: Damballa (or Dan) Wèdo, symbolized by the snake and the rainbow; Aïson; Sogbo, a member of the Dahomean thunder pantheon; Kébioso (Hevioso in Dahomey), another important deity of the thunder pantheon; Agwé, a deity of the sea; Nananbouloucou, a *loa* of herbs and medicine (in Dahomey, the ancestor of all deities, and parent of Mawu and Lisa, from whom all *vodouns* are descended); Legba, guardian of the gateway and the crossroads, and the messenger through whom all appeals to the deities must be addressed; Azaka Médé, spirit of a stream which the dead must cross; Marassa, deity of twins; Loko, a major deity of the sky pantheon; and Agasu (in Dahomey, the panther fetish, of special significance to the royal family). The *loa* who come from Yoruba tradition include Ogoun, Chango (Shango), Obatalá and others already mentioned in connection with Yoruba rites in Trinidad and Cuba.

There has been some, but not an excessive, intrusion of Catholic practices and doctrine into Vodoun. Many of the *loa* are identified with Catholic saints. Sometimes a so-called *prêt' savane*, an unordained individual, will read or recite Catholic prayers to begin a service for the dead, or some other ritual. Beyond these elements, and the fact that saints are invoked among the *loa*, there is little in the Vodoun service to remind us that Vodoun and Catholicism have lived intimately side by side for centuries. God (called Bondieu) has a place in Vodoun, but is considered a force apart, positioned at the very apex of all the pantheons and other powers. He is regarded as the supreme source of all things. But he is less immediate to man than are the *loa*. He is invoked along with the *loa* and the dead, but he is thought of as being something like Fa — destiny — in Dahomean belief.

When an action is required to help a family or an individual, or when the supernatural must be placated, it is the *loa* and the dead who are appealed to. While God is the supreme force, he is not the total force. For many Vodounists, God occupies a niche much like that of Nyame, the Ashanti Sky God, or of Olorun, paramount *orisha* of the Yoruba.

The conditions that were congenial to the survival of Vodoun in Haitian life were various. Among the more important was the fact that when the French were evicted by the Revolution, the population of Haiti was almost entirely of African descent. It was largely homogeneous in race and (in the broad aspects) in culture. The timing of the Revolution was also important as regards cultural development and survivals. Vodoun was alive and flourishing at that moment, and with the diminishing of European influences there was a diminution of pressures against the so-called "pagan" practices. It was also significant that the major Christian influence in Haiti was the Catholic Church rather than the Protestant. While the Catholic Church sought to wean the Haitians away from Vodoun, it followed a rather permissive policy through the years, expectant that exposure to Christian teaching would in time make Vodoun archaic. It encouraged (or accepted) syncretisms such as giving various *loa* the personalities of Catholic saints, and identifying Legba with Satan. Another factor was the identification that various Haitian leaders had with Vodoun. And above all, there was the fact that Vodoun was a comprehensive system of belief that affected all aspects of life, for which Catholic belief was not an adequate substitute.

In 1814, during Christophe's reign in the north, the area under his control is said to have had only three priests. During Boyer's administration, 1818-1843, Catholicism was the official state religion, but there were still few priests, and the President acted as chief of the Church in Haiti. The sociologist Leyburn noted:

> Every effort of the state failing to provide proper religious leadership, Boyer resigned himself to permitting those who professed to be priests to practice in the republic. There were seventy so-called priests in the country in 1840. Some of them had once been in the holy orders, but had been unfrocked; they found in Haiti not only a haven but a fertile field for gain. In addition to these religious renegades came adventurers who knew just enough of ritual and theology to use the priestly garb as a cover for easy graft . . . . They baptised houses, boats and doorposts, and blessed fetish charms or amulets, all for a fee.[5]

It was not until 1860, after the death of the Emperor Soulouque, that Haiti signed a concordat with the Roman Church. Thus it can be seen that for the first sixty or more years of Haitian independence Catholic influence

was weak and sporadic. Those years were crucial in preserving, crystalliz-
ing, and hardening the form of Vodoun. Because the ways of Haitian life
have not changed much in the past century, Vodoun, which touches on so
many aspects of daily living, also has remained largely unchanged.

Following the Revolution, Haiti became an agrarian society, echo-
ing life on the African continent. As agrarians, Haitians tended to be conservative. They sought to protect traditional ways, religious and secular, and
the freedoms that go with agrarian life and independence, just as they sought
to preserve ownership of their small plots of land. Vodoun survived for some
of the same reasons that various other cultural institutions survived, among
them *plaçage* (the custom which permitted a man to have several wives, one
on each separate landholding), the cooperative work group (the *coumbite*),
the pre-Easter Rara festivities, and the harvest festivals.

The experience of African-derived societies in the British controlled
islands of the Caribbean was different in serveral noteworthy respects. In
Jamaica, for example, there was an unbroken continuity of British control
and influence, a population that was not exclusively of African derivation,
and a constant pressure toward Christianization. Jamaica today is predominantly English and Christian in culture. What is perhaps most remarkable is
that African tradition has survived in Jamaica even to the extent it has, and
disguised or watered-down aspects of African religious custom are still to be
found at all.

4 THE SOCIAL AND POLITICAL SIGNIFICANCE OF VODOUN

The role that Vodoun has played in Haiti's political life has never
been clearly defined. Many legends credit cult leaders with heroic actions
against the French both before and during the Haitian Revolution. Implicit
or explicit in these legends is the belief that the cults generated the motivation, the passion, and even the frenzy required for patriotic sacrifice and
achievement. It is said, for example, that a cult leader named Makandal was
responsible for an abortive rebellion against the French in 1757. Rites conducted by Boukman, a *houngan* at Bois Caiman, are reputed to have incited
the first blow of the Revolution against the French planters in 1791. French

chroniclers of the period were fond of stressing the superstition and witchcraft of the Haitians, the magic charms and rites which the Blacks used to
make themselves invincible and invulnerable to bullets. But the Revolution
was not fought with or motivated by witchcraft. The armies of Toussaint,
Dessalines, and Christophe fought against great odds with the conventional
weapons of war and with determination, bravery, and hatred of the
colonialists.

Vodoun and witchcraft undoubtedly lurked on the periphery of the
conflict, but they were not at its center as some European chroniclers sug-
gested. Most Haitians then, as now, probably were attached to the African
cults. No doubt many were ardent Vodounists. But Vodoun was not an
organization that could be manipulated by an individual or a group. There
was no paramount chief. The Vodoun cults were small *sociétés* of rural or
urban people, nothing more.

The triumverate of revolutionary leaders in the north, L'Ouverture,
Dessalines, and Christophe, nevertheless recognized the potential of the
cults to stir up disorder. Each of them during his time in power sought to
control and limit cult activities. Later, a number of nineteenth century leaders were reputed to have had connections with the cults. This may well have
been, in some cases, merely recognition on the part of leaders that the cults
could in some way be an influence in politics. Some, like Soulouque who
came to power in 1843 and then made himself Emperor, were emotionally
and culturally tied to Vodoun. Antoine Simon, who became President in
1908, also was known to be a Vodounist. In the main, however, it is not
clear whether certain leaders were *aficionados* of African cult activities,
interested only casually, politically motivated, or totally aloof. Much of the
"evidence" against Presidents alleged to be practicing Vodounists comes
out of legend or folklore. For example, there is an old song which memor-
ializes a march of cultists to the National Palace in the time of President
Borno. Borno was alleged to be much influenced by Afro-Haitian cult beliefs. According to legend, a group of *houngans* and their followers swarmed
to the Palace grounds one day and refused to leave until Borno sent money
out to them as tribute to Gèdé, the spirit of the cemetery. The song goes, in
part:

> Papa Gèdé is a handsome fellow.
> Gèdé Nimbo is a handsome fellow.
> He is all dressed in black,
> For he goes to the Palace.

Many Haitian political figures have been tarred with Vodoun by their
enemies. In this sense, Vodoun sometimes has been an issue, but there is
no evidence that the cults have ever controlled or had great influence in the
Palace. Vodoun has perhaps had the same meaning to some Haitian leaders

as astrology has had to some leaders in India.

The assumption that *houngans* of prestige could have political power or influence in their own regions is, of course, reasonable. One cult leader by the name of Mérisier is memorialized in several songs. He lived in the south, in the region of Jacmel, during the administration of President Florvil Hippolyte in the last decade of the nineteenth century. Hippolyte apparently regarded Mérisier as a dangerous political enemy, and the region of Jacmel as an area of potential revolution. Soberly written history says merely that on a certain day in 1896 Hippolyte "decided to undertake a long journey to Jacmel."[6] The oral history of folklore declares that the purpose of the trip was to seize Mérisier and sack the town of Jacmel. Hippolyte died of a stroke enroute, and folklore has it that this denouement was the result of Mérisier's magic.

The question of Vodoun's influence in politics in earlier days is blurred or distorted for a variety of reasons. European writers sometimes were unaware of Vodoun as a genuine religious pattern common to the entire nation, and, as we have noted, frequently delighted in depicting the superstitious character of the people. Haitian historians of the past were sensitive to the charge that the country was overrun with pagan rites, and they largely avoided mention of Vodoun. Little on the subject is likely to be found in government archives for much the same reason.

However, there is somewhat more light on the contemporary situation in which the country finds itself under the harsh rule of François Duvalier. A practicing physician who had attended an American university, Duvalier took power in 1957, when the political situation was so badly deteriorated that it seemed virtually impossible to form a stable government. Duvalier had the backing of both the liberal elements and the commercial class. In addition, he had shown a tolerant and largely intellectual interest in Vodoun, as evidenced by his activities in connection with the Bureau of Ethnology; this open-minded attitude brought support from elements of the intelligentsia (Vodoun as an aspect of Haitian tradition and folklore had over the previous twenty or thirty years become *arrivé* among these people) and perhaps from the cults as well. Duvalier's transformation from a mild-mannered physician into an ambitious, iron-fisted dictator who in effect declared himself permanent ruler of the nation surprised most of those who had supported him. He struck boldly at all sources of power — the commercial class, the Catholic Church, the intelligentsia, and the army — and weakened or destroyed any social or political elements that might possibly contest his control of the nation. Where did Vodoun fit in this picture? In the beginning, Duvalier's intellectual and cultural interest in Vodoun had been twisted by his enemies into a familiar accusation — that he was a Vodounist himself, and that he proposed to revitalize Vodoun and give it a special place of honor. While these charges might well have alienated some political support, they probably convinced many among the peasantry that Duvalier would be a champion of Afro-Haitian cult beliefs that had for so long been contemned among the elite and frequently harassed by the Catholic Church and the state. The peasants believed that in Duvalier they had the perennially-sought "Black president" who would protect their interests. His harsh treatment of the high ranking clergy of the Catholic and Episcopal Churches in Haiti for their critical attitudes toward his ruthless measures possibly reinforced this impression.

From all the facts that are readily available, it appears that Duvalier has simultaneously cut down the influence of Christian clergy and consolidated his control over Vodoun. The Afro-Haitian cults now have enhanced prestige, but it is clear that they are dependent upon the President. The controls Duvalier exercises over Vodoun are political, but they make him, in effect, the head of a socio-religious institution that rarely has had a single nerve center. His controls over Vodoun have been exercised in the same manner as his controls over other elements in Haitian life. *Houngans* who cooperate are in good standing. Those who do not are in jeopardy, and there have been reports that some who have not played the game by his rules have been jailed or assassinated, or have simply disappeared.

Whatever the truth of these reports, it seems clear that Duvalier had the ability to recognize Vodoun as a stubborn, traditional, and effective institution of social organization in the countryside. In utilizing the cults as a ready-made tool to help accomplish his purposes (whatever those purposes may be in addition to retention of power), he has made obvious what should have been obvious to other presidents before him. A quality Duvalier possesses that others have not possessed is that of not caring for the good opinion of the elite and the outside world. He has attached himself to and used Vodoun openly. One could not profitably speculate on how long this state of affairs might last. On the negative side (from Duvalier's point of view) is the fact that the Haitian *habitant's* economic condition has deteriorated progressively, and at some critical moment this will be consciously weighed against the seeming security Duvalier has extended to the cults.

One is tempted to speculate on what social and economic reforms might be accomplished through intelligent and benevolent use of the Vodoun cult centers by a progress-minded government. In the southland of the United States for many years the Negro church was the main contact point of the Negro community. The church was the center of social organization and cooperation. It was used not only for religious purposes but for educational projects. In the church there were meetings to discuss local problems (later on, national problems), or to listen to experts on agriculture or chicken raising or health matters. It was no accident that when the civil rights movement materialized in the southern states, ministers of the churches provided the main leadership. This phenomenon was also clearly observable in the northern urban centers. The typical Haitian cult is a community center headed by a *houngan* or a *mambo* whose words carry great weight. The transformation of this center into a place where fundamental educative processes, as well as religious rites, could be carried on could vitally affect the nation's welfare. Health rules and precautions, agricultural advice, elemental literacy, sound management of income and acreage, all these things could be taught or at least stimulated. The basic organization already exists. And so far it has never been used by the state except for political advantage.

One obvious difficulty in transforming the local cults into centers of cultural advance is that among the cult priests only a relative few are moderately educated. Many are literate, many more half-literate or non-literate. They have mastered a system of thought and tradition which can be eroded only by cultural advance and larger public horizons. They have a stake in traditional ways, and a considerable and largely justifiable distrust of the state. Nevertheless, the *houngan* is called upon by his followers for many kinds of advice. Ostensibly relaying opinions of the ancestors and judgments of the *loa*, he even now calls attention to crops that are not being properly cared for, lax work habits, and poor community cooperation, and he frequently assigns reasons for sickness and crop failure. With good indoctrination in matters of health, agriculture, and community welfare, he could play a vital part in healing the sick society without suffering any diminution in prestige. His task would be larger, but a conscientious *houngan* might also find his long-term rewards larger if he were able to better understand and convey, in modern terms, some of the immediate causes of poor crops, ill health, and various other sufferings which traditionally are explained as ill will or whimsy on the part of the *loa*, the dead, and other spirits.

We have seen that Vodoun is conservative, that it is a repository of old beliefs, that it has an internal dynamic, and that it is a system of organization of known and unknown forces. If it has had more meaning to most Haitians than Christian doctrine, it is because Christianity has seemed to offer only doctrine and guidelines to behavior, whereas Vodoun offers doctrine, social controls, a pattern of family relations, direct communication with original forces, emotional release, dance, music, meaningful socializing, drama, theater, legend and folklore, motivation, alternatives to threatening dangers, individual initiatives through placation and invocation, treatment of ailments by means of herb lotions and rituals, protection of fields, fertility, and a continuing familiar relationship with the ancestors.

So although Haitians have been willing to accept Catholicism, they have been unwilling to leave Vodoun behind. Those who have accepted one or another of the Protestant faiths have had to give up everything related to Vodoun — not only their amulets, drums, and sacred stones, but dancing (in some cases even pure social dancing), traditional songs, and participation in a vast variety of social affairs related to the *hounfor*. They must not turn to the *houngan* for advice, for medical treatment, for protections against the unknown. They must avoid the all-important gatherings of the extended family to pay respect to the *loa* and the ancestors; the harvest rituals when the rice and yams are brought in; the rituals of the fishermen to call and placate the *loa* of the sea. In short, to attain what some Christian cults offer, they must give up nearly everything that makes life bearable in a hostile environment. Some have said that it is Vodoun that has kept the nation backward. But it appears to be the contrary that is true: Vodoun has survived because the country is backward, because no satisfactory alternatives are available. Christianity long ago would have proved more meaningful to the Haitian peasant if it had somehow been able to offer an integrated *system* that could substitute for the *system* of which Vodoun is a part. But Christian doctrine must be grafted onto an already existing social phenomenon, and without Vodoun the Haitian would largely lack the explanations, answers, meanings, comforts, and relationships that it provides. If Christian doctrine could be offered in combination with education, health care, better rewards for hard labor, rising expectations, alternative activities that would satisfy emotional and creative needs, and so on, Vodoun would not, it is almost certain, remain the force in Haitian life that it is today. The failure is not that of Vodoun, which provides something essential. The failure is that of the society at large, which has provided no other satisfactory choices.

This failure is not merely the result of divergent class interests (as between the elite and the peasantry), inept or calloused government, the conservatism of the peasantry, or willful disregard of the long-drawn-out economic duress of most of the population. These elements have been particularly discernible in certain periods of Haitian history. But there have also been governments that have attempted, in different ways, to move the Haitian society forward. And there is every evidence that many *habitants* of the countryside would go along with and encourage meaningful change if given the opportunity. But the question of where and how to begin staggers the mind. New agricultural methods, with ample supplies of fertilizers? But how could these be applied to tiny garden plots scattered over rocky mountain terrain? Combination of isolated plots into large fields that could be cooperatively worked? There is already an institution for cooperative effort that can deal more effectively with mountainside plots, and in the plains the amount of peasant landholdings is limited. New tools with which to work the soil? The plow is useless except in the alluvial valleys. New roads and better access to the urban centers, and new methods of marketing various produce? The benefits would be limited. If all of these things together doubled the per capita Haitian income, it would amount to no more than fifty dollars a year. Double the amount of land available to each peasant? There is no more tillable land to give out. Emigration has been recommended to relieve the population pressure, but few have the resources to emigrate, and at best the process would keep the population stable at its present level, which is not good enough. Furthermore, the immigration policies of neighboring countries, which have their own problems, are not congenial to an influx of unskilled, illiterate workers. When one considers the enormous efforts that Puerto Rico and Cuba have made, and the large residue of poverty still left in those places, one can get a glimmering of what would be required in Haiti. It seems to this observer that Haiti will never even begin to find its way out of the economic morass without industrialization and systematic exploitation of such natural resources as it may have. And these developments do not now appear on the horizon. The situation is in fact so desperate that even radical political movements are not particularly eager to take over control, for there appear to be limited possibilities for greatly bettering the life of the nation. Some day, nevertheless, a start will have to be made.

If Haitian governments have not been able to provide economic answers, neither has Vodoun. The failure of the secular and political society (and one might add, the failure of the Christian churches to take a larger view) is what keeps Vodoun meaningful and alive for so many Haitians.

Although we tend to see Vodoun as *hounfor*-centered, we must not neglect to perceive the extent to which it is family-centered. Rituals and observances of many kinds can and are held without the participation of a *houngan,* and sometimes a *houngan* is present not out of necessity but as a means of leaving out nothing that might enhance a ceremony or family activity. The force of Vodoun has been significant at the family level, strengthening family ties and keeping alive a system of organization that has made life tolerable within a larger society that has neglected the individual and his needs.

For the elite, Vodoun has often been an embarrassment and a tribulation. They have felt the need to apologize for its existence, to deplore its existence, even to deny its existence. They have tended to equate it with the darkness of race, without really perceiving that it helps to satisfy essential social needs for which the elite, so often in political power, have never been able to supply more than superficial answers. As for the intelligentsia, it is only in recent decades that they have embraced Vodoun as the great manifestation of Haitian tradition. Until at least the middle 1930's, there were few among the intellectuals who did not look elsewhere, to the United States and Europe, for stimulation, ideas, and causes. The poet and novelist Jacques Roumain was one of those who first saw clearly, during this period, that the culture of the elite was in many respects a sterile transplant from France, and that the peasant heritage of Vodoun, with its extended meanings, was the real culture of Haiti. Other Haitian writers had dealt with the subject, and some of them had made exceedingly worthwhile studies of certain aspects of Vodoun, of oral literature, the Creole language, and Haitian tradition in general. Some had been motivated by a desire to see their culture objectively, and to dispel old cliches. Others seemed to have had among their motives, subconscious or not, a desire to create a Haitian mystique and to demonstrate that the Haitian had special qualities of his own. The *mouvement folklorique* was something different. It determined to embráce Haitian tradition. Heroes of the new literature were peasants, and Vodoun was the setting. The so-called "renaissance" in art (in reality a new development, for there was little precedent in tradition) was a specialized aspect of the *mouvement folklorique*. Untaught painters had brushes put in their hands, and were provided with canvas and paint. Out of this "renaissance" there came some spectacular primitive painting. Faces of Haitian peasants and village scenes looked down from the walls of government buildings, hotels, and the Episcopal Cathedral Sainte-Trinité. The Centre d'Art had a seemingly endless supply of primitive paintings to sell. Vodoun rites were depicted, the *loa* of Vodoun were portrayed. The pre-Easter Rara festival, peasant version, appeared in countless paintings. Thus the painters (many of them of peasant origin) also had discovered and projected the essence of the nation. Haitian and foreign scholars of the 1940's and 1950's, including anthropologists, sociologists, musicologists, and folklorists, focused their attention on Vodoun. Serious Haitian musicians (at least two, possibly more) wrote serious compositions based on traditional Vodoun songs. Choral groups (recruited from both the elite and peasant classes) sang repertoires of authentic (though arranged) Vodoun songs for tourists, overseas audiences, and records. Vodoun even infiltrated the popular music of the country. It was all acceptable now and desirable. Vodoun was intellectualized and emotionalized. And yet, all this did little to change the institution of Vodoun or to better the status or condition of those for whom Vodoun was a system of life. As Rémy Bastien observes with keen insight in his discussion in this publication, "The Haitian *clercs* mistook their passionate interest in folklore for the active care they should have taken of their illiterate brothers."

This is much where the situation rests today. The intellectuals have made Vodoun respectable in the arts. The Church waits for a time when Vodoun will be banished or eroded. Those who at this moment control the state use Vodoun as a political instrument to help preserve their power. And Vodoun itself remains little changed, certainly no weaker, than a half century ago. It makes heavy demands, exacts conformity, and leads its followers through a maze of cause and effect that is the scorn of the educated and the Western-oriented. But it is meaningful, offers a sense of community and social diversion, provides at one time a world of unseen dangers and security against those dangers, and keeps tight the knot that binds together the extended peasant family.

FOOTNOTES

(References cited here may be found in the Annotated Bibliography)

1. The word *Vodoun* has appeared in many spellings over the past century and a half, and no standard orthography has yet been agreed upon. Writers and anthropologists in the twentieth century have used the following spellings: Melville J. Herskovits—*Vodu* and *Vodun;* George Eaton Simpson—*Vodun* (after an earlier trial of *Vôdoun);* Odette Menneson Rigaud—*Vodou;* Milo Rigaud—*Voudoo;* Robert A. Hall, Jr.—*Vaudoun;* Selden Rodman—*Vaudou;* Maya Deren—*Voudoun;* Eugène Aubin—*Vaudoux;* James Leyburn—*Vodun;* Alfred Métraux—*Voodoo;* the publications of the Haitian Bureau d'Ethnologie—*Vodou;* and Harold Courlander—*Vodoun.* It has always seemed to me that the spelling *Vodoun* most accurately represents the Haitian pronunciation (French phonetics), and I have stayed with it since 1939. In the absence of any general agreement among the specialists, there can hardly be any real quarrel about this choice.

2. The entire island, as distinguished from its two parts, the Republic of Haiti and the Dominican Republic, has been called, variously, Haiti, Hispaniola, and Santo Domingo. These confusions are inherited from colonial times, and contemporary maps continue to be at odds with one another on the subject. The Indians of Columbus' time are said to have called the island Haiti. The Spanish dubbed the island Hispaniola. Later, the Spanish called the eastern two-thirds of the island Santo Domingo,

and the French referred to their western third as Saint-Domingue. Following the Haitian Revolution, the western third was again called by its original name, Haiti.

3. Until only a few decades ago, Protestant sects had virtually no influence in Haiti. In recent years, Methodists, Baptists, Wesleyans, Jehovah's Witnesses and other Protestant groups have been estimated to have a total following of 8 or 10 percent of the population. The other 90 percent, of course, is at least nominally Catholic.

4. The author has compiled a list of 221 *loa* identified with Anago-Arada and related rites, and 77 *loa* belonging to the Congo and Pétro cycle. Other observers also have provided comprehensive lists. Many of those named as distinct *loa* are manifestations of another deity. There are large families of Ogouns, Changos, and Gèdés, for example. See Courlander, 1960, pp. 317 ff.

5. Leyburn, 1945, p. 123.

6. Léger, 1907, p. 246 in the French edition; p. 248 in the English translation.

1

General Toussaint L'Ouverture. [Courtesy of the Pan American Union.]

2

General Jean-Jacques Dessalines. [Courtesy of the Pan American Union.]

3   Deforestation of a Haitian landscape. The trees have been cut primarily for fuel. [Photo from the United Nations.]

4

A small settlement on a mountain slope near Kenscoff in southern Haiti. [Photo by John Scofield © National Geographic Society.]

5 Section of line village on the road to Jeremie in southern Haiti. The walls of the houses are unplastered, showing the technique of pole and lath construction. In the fronts are the concrete coffee-drying floors built en masse several years ago in a countrywide campaign. [Photo by Richard P. Schaedel.]

6 A peasant home in a hill village near St. Raphaël in northern Haiti. Seed corn hangs from the frame on the left. [Photo © National Geographic Society.]

7 Peasant houses near Les Cayes, southern Haiti. These two-room houses have plastered walls and *tonnelle* (porch) indicative of relatively modest status. [Photo by Richard P. Schaedel.]

8 Bamboo rafts for carrying market produce to weekly regional Marfranc market. Rafts are dismantled after each trip as they cannot be propelled upstream against the current. [Photo by Richard P. Schaedel.]

9 Farm women going to market. [Photo from the International Labor Organization through the Pan American Union.]

10 Small, daily local roadside market in southern Haiti. Except for the butchers, no men participate. [Photo by Richard P. Schaedel.]

11

The Iron Market in Port-au-Prince.
[Photo by John Scofield © National
Geographic Society.]

12 Waterfront market in the La Saline district of Port-au-Prince. Wood for charcoal is piled along the dock, and a boat is being repaired in the background. Most of the vendors at this market are from the countryside. [Photo by John Scofield © National Geographic Society.]

13

A conch-shell trumpet is blown to call a *coumbite*. [Photo by Harold Courlander.]

14   Haitian drummers. The designs on the drums resemble the ritual drawings (vèvès) made during Vodoun services. [Photo from the Pan American Union.]

Haitian murals in the Episcopal Cathedral Sainte-Trinité, Port-au-Prince. [Photo © National Geographic Society.]   15

Altar in a *hounfor* in Port-au-Prince. The deity, or *loa*, is represented by the cross and skull. [Photo by Harold Courlander.] **16**

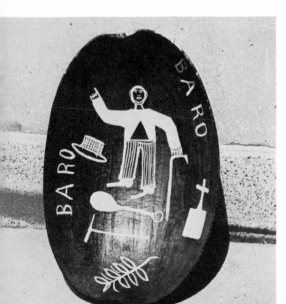

17

Inner surface of a ritual bowl made from a calabash and painted black and white. The figure and the other articles represent Baron Samedi, a "dead" *loa* of the graveyard. [Photo by Harold Courlander.]

VODOUN AND POLITICS IN HAITI

by Rémy Bastien

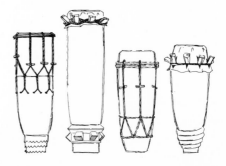

VODOUN AND POLITICS IN HAITI

by Rémy Bastien

INTRODUCTION

Attitudes toward Vodoun have varied with the political fortunes of Haiti. As the nation has grappled with changing dictatorships and never-ending poverty, its plight has not been met with sympathy. The stern criticisms and virtually defamatory press campaigns which have been aimed at weakening a prevailing government, have focused their attacks on Vodoun, only to slander the nation as a whole. In much the same way Vodoun has been used to justify the actions of foreign or domestic powers. Over the span of a few years, Vodoun may be revealed as orgiastic or felicific, magical or cannibalistic, esthetic or entertaining. In short, Vodoun is an institution which lends itself to contradictory interpretations, all of which are partially correct.

A few examples will illustrate the somewhat occult relation between the depiction of Vodoun and the political situation in Haiti. Given the date of publication of an essay on Vodoun and knowing the contemporary state of affairs in Haiti or of the international conjuncture we can guess what the author's general orientation will be. We may judge the writers of the nineteenth century as myopic and tainted with selfrighteousness. We may fail to see, however, that we are victims of our own prejudices, of the commanding interests of our times, and of our professional training. Furthermore, the "right" type of writer always appears at the "right" moment regardless of whether he hopes to exploit the opportunity for fame and gain or desires to serve a cause.

We shall draw our examples from a fairly recent period in Haitian history. In 1915, following severe political troubles, the Marines landed and the country was occupied by the United States. The sins of anarchy and insolvability were not enough to justify what was in fact aggression against an infinitely weaker opponent. No doubt Haiti was in turmoil. Yet during the next fifteen years or so no effort was spared to convince the American public that a country in which such abominations took place during the "voodoo" ceremonies could find its salvation only through occupation. Craige, Niles, and Seabrook, among others, oblivious of all critical sense, played the role of directors and soothers of conscience.

From the middle thirties onward, under the conciliating influence of the Good Neighbor Policy and in opposition to the intolerance of Fascism, a new breed of essayists came forth. Its members were chiefly social scientists trained in the traditions of cultural relativism and objective analysis. Their works superseded the sensationalist writing of the former period, and Vodoun became a popular religion worthy of respect. Moreover, instead of being the central topic of study, Vodoun was rightly regarded as only one of the many elements composing the Haitian way of life. Herskovits and Leyburn remain the outstanding individuals in the new phase of studies.

The metamorphosis went even further after World War II with the rapid advance of nationalism in Africa and Asia and the search for new values. At that time Haiti was experiencing one of its too rare periods of relative prosperity and consequently the metaphysics of Vodoun were "discovered." Deren, Rigaud, and Jahn discoursed at length on the hierarchy of forces, on esoteric tradition, on cosmic and psychic orders. The evolution was complete: from diabolism and obscenity to ethics and philosophy.

But Vodoun is condemned to a continual rise and fall. After 1960, the excesses and intractability of President Duvalier started a new cycle, the horrible crept back into the press and we read of gory offerings, of human sacrifices performed in the very basement of the National Palace in Port-au-Prince. Seabrook is back.

Where does the truth lie? We can answer better after analyzing what Vodoun is and trying to establish its role not only in Haitian politics but also in the health, economics, and group relations of the country.

1 ORIGINS AND GROWTH OF VODOUN

If we accept the word as generic, Vodoun is no monopoly of Haiti. As a popular religion that syncretized a variety of African cults and Christian elements, it has a broad following in Brazil, was well-entrenched in Cuba, and took a variety of forms in Jamaica; some of its manifestations have been found in Louisiana. Its distribution means that it cropped up in the territories of the main colonial powers, French, Spanish, British, and Portuguese, irrespective of the dominant Catholicism or Protestantism of the metropolises. Its appearance was due to two circumstances created by Negro slavery: (1) the failure of Christianity to provide the Africans with a satisfactory religious life, and (2) the resistance of the African to his lot, and his will to preserve as much of his cultural heritage as possible. Whereas the Spanish colonists had some success in applying missionary methods to the conversion of the great nuclei of Amerindian population in Mesoamerica and the Andean area, the plantation owners in the West Indies, Brazil, and the southern United States did not care to reconcile human exploitation and the quick-profit mentality with religious fervor. The French colonists were known for their lack of religiosity. Elsewhere religious teaching was frowned upon by the masters and, at least before Abolition, the ministers found little incentive to include the slaves among their flocks. No doubt the Jesuits in Haiti (or rather Saint-Domingue) did show some spirit in opening schools for the Negroes but their work was short-lived; expulsion followed soon after. Equally limited were the efforts of Baptists and Moravian Brethren in Jamaica.[1]

Meager as it was, the presence of Christianity was enough to impress the slaves. They borrowed elements from its ritual and dogma and blended them with their own African heritage. The syncretized Afro-religions of the New World simultaneously practiced both Vodoun and Catholicism, with surprising ease at times. While the economic system of the dominant Europeans created tension, antagonism, and violence, the religious system of the slaves successfully created a workable pattern of coexistence. Religious coexistence, however, did not exclude resistance on the political plane. The eradication of their social and political organization did not deter the Africans from trying to regain their freedom. Their attempts, failures, and rare triumphs are an inseparable part of the struggle for liberty in the Americas, be it in the Palmares in Brazil, the southern part of Dutch Guiana, Jamaica, Mexico, or Haiti. What is of interest to us is the role that magic and religion played in the conflict. Data may be scarce in many cases but its abundance in the history of Haiti allows us to suppose that elsewhere the rebellious leaders used similar methods to fire the imagination and sustain the courage of their followers.

From this it can be seen that the magico-religious complex practiced by the slaves—we may as well call it Vodoun—contained both a social character and a secret or political one. Chroniclers of the eighteenth century often noted the religious dances performed by Negroes on the plantations. Such gatherings were tolerated and at times encouraged by the colonists. Parallel to these open manifestations were the secret meetings of Vodoun adepts whose primary purpose was not to find an outlet to the frustrations of servile life through dancing, but to create cohesion among the participants in plots against the existing social order. We are ready to concede that the religious side of such meetings was incidental to their political goals, but the fact cannot be denied that Vodoun was the cement which bound the members of the conspiracy and that it served as a catalyst when the time for action came.

In the French colony of Saint-Domingue, later known as Haiti, magico-religious power was one of the attributes of many slave leaders. Makandal manipulated poison as successfully as he convinced his followers that he could fade out of sight at will; he was burned alive in 1758. Later, in 1791 a general uprising of slaves was led by Boukman, a powerful man and a Vodoun priest, as well as a *metteur en scène* of no ordinary talent. A week before the outbreak of the revolt which eventually led to the independence of Haiti, he gathered his closest affiliates in a clearing of the Bois Caiman. There, under a raging tropical downpour accompanied by lightning and the cracking of giant trees, he performed a Pétro ceremony. A pig was sacrificed and its blood, mixed with gunpowder, was distributed among participants to strengthen their will to win. Boukman soon was killed in an encounter with the disciplined French forces, but his task was successfully accomplished by new leaders who, unlike Boukman, possessed military genius and little faith in Vodoun.

We mentioned the word Pétro. It refers to one of the two main Vodoun rites, Rada and Pétro. According to an opinion fairly current among believers, but which may not be entirely correct, the two rites have quite distinct origins. The Rada gods, or *loas,* came from Africa and their role during the slavery period was one of appeasers and conformists, giving solace to their "children." The Pétro were born in Haiti and some of them were deified priests and leaders. They were bent on action through fire, poison, and massacre. While Vodoun tradition piously holds that both groups united to guide the faithful to freedom, it also points out the goodness of the Rada in contrast to the violence and addiction to magic of their younger rivals, the Pétro. The contrast may be exaggerated, but one may wonder if it does not in its simplicity reveal the dual character of Vodoun referred to above. Moreover, it is possible that the two rites hold sway alternately over Haitian life and especially over politics according to the circumstances — crisis or peace. Magic, violence, and secrecy are called for on the one hand; piety, conciliation, and thanksgiving on the other.

Many foreign authors have deplored the high price Haiti had to pay for its independence: the quasi-total destruction of the colonial irrigation system, the wrecking of the sugar refineries, the burning of the plantations. But these are material losses. Perhaps more important was the isolation both imposed upon and chosen by the new country. Surrounded by slave colonies, Haiti became a black sheep. Furthermore, the nation's first ruler, Dessalines, concerned about a possible return of the French, decided to maintain only limited commercial relations with the outside world. At one time he even considered razing all the coastal cities except a few seaports and concentrating the decimated population in the mountains where defense would be easier. Haiti's cultural isolation was made acute when the white settlers, whose technological knowledge could have helped greatly in rebuilding the former colony's economic wealth on a non-slavery basis, either fled or were killed. Lastly and most important for the history of Vodoun, the severance of all ties with France meant that the Holy See would neither establish relations with the new republic nor provide for the spiritual needs of its inhabitants for nearly sixty years. It was not until 1860 that the Haitian Government, after repeated efforts, succeeded in signing a concordat with the Vatican. In the interim, defrocked prelates of dubious morality together with downright impostors posing as priests catered to the magical tastes of the peasantry, thus reinforcing the already existing familiarity between Vodoun and Catholicism.

By 1860, a major date in the religious history of the country, Haiti was already facing most of the socio-cultural problems of today. Blacks and mulattos, at odds since colonial times, were fighting for power. Schools were scarce and illiteracy undoubtedly stood where it stands today, above 85 percent. Constitutions and laws were written in French, a language intelligible only to the educated minority. Health conditions were bad. Roads were almost nonexistent and goods were carried either on the heads of women or by coastal shipping. Attempts to create a landed gentry, Black and mulatto, controlling a cheap labor force had failed. This did not mean, how-

ever, that large estates disappeared completely; a small number of them survived under the ownership of King Christophe's former aristocrats in the
north. There were others in the Cul-de-Sac near Port-au-Prince and in the
southern peninsula. But they were to be found chiefly in the lowlands where
control, both by the proprietors and the government, was easier.

Yet, the owners did not have their hearts in the business. In the manner of the French colonists they did not live on their estates and they displayed little interest in agricultural innovations to increase productivity.
With typical *latifundista* disdain, they considered their estates to be merely a
source of revenues which allowed them to enjoy the dubious comforts of
Haitian urban life, participate in political intrigue, and educate their sons
in Paris. Those who were educated studied the humanities which prepared
them for liberal professions, not engineering or agronomy which could have
helped them attack the land problems of the nation.

Nevertheless, the state did try to apply an agricultural policy that was
simple and to the point: increase the production of exportable goods. Land
grants were made on the condition that such goods would be cultivated. The
lack of technicians, however, plus a restive labor force, and poor administration, frustrated these efforts.

In sum, the peasant won his battle against the big landowner and the
plantation system. At that time, however, the economy of the country rested
on a firmer basis than it does today. Land was plentiful for a population of
less than a million. Haitian coffee and cotton had few competitors; molasses
and dyewood found a sure market in Europe. Since there was no industrialization, urban development was practically nil and the overwhelming
majority of the population lived in hamlets or on isolated farms. Vodoun,
occasionally persecuted but tolerated or encouraged most of the time, had
put its stamp on all facets of peasant life. Such, then, was the general picture
facing the first members of the Catholic clergy who landed in Haiti after the
Concordat of 1860.

As Alfred Métraux[2] rightly states, however, the Catholic Church
showed lack of discernment in coping with the situation confronting it.
Since it was well known that the rural masses were attached to "fetichism
and superstitions" (in the vocabulary of the time) and that they should be
enlightened and brought to the true Faith, this was obviously a task for missionaries. They would have to fight illiteracy, sickness, and "pagan" practices, and provide both physical and spiritual care. Instead, the Church
nicely divided the country into parishes on the French model. This division
resulted in an undue concentration of priests in the urban areas while the
rural population was neglected. Nor were the priests particularly well prepared for missionary work. If some of them displayed devotion and sacrifice

in the performance of their duty, others became the victims of apathy and routine. Some even neglected to learn Creole, the language spoken by all Haitians.

A final point must be made clear in order to understand the subsequent relations between Church, state, and Vodoun, as we discuss them. The majority of the Catholic clergy of Haiti until this time had been of foreign origin and, for linguistic purposes, mostly French. The clergy which was soon to become a political force was entrusted with a secret mission: to create a climate of opinion favorable to a voluntary association of Haiti with France. It is only too well known that in the nineteenth century missionaries in Africa and Asia were often the spearhead of economic penetration and colonial rule. It is not strange, then, that patriotic Frenchmen would undertake to combine faith with national glory. In order to carry out the scheme, the French clerics concentrated on the education of the upper class. They opened excellent secondary schools where Haitian students were fully indoctrinated in the grandeur of France and exposed to insinuations about the backwardness of their country and its incapacity for self-rule.

The plan failed and was given up in the late 1890's. But the imported clergy, conservative as usual, maintained an informal alliance with the upper class whose education and interests tended to set it apart from the rest of the population. Little wonder that by 1960 the clergy of Haiti openly took the side of the bourgeoisie. This led the opponent (in this case the government) to take stern measures against the alliance of the bourgeoisie and the clergy, and in the name of nationalism, to look for support from the masses and Vodoun.

2 BELIEFS AND STRUCTURE OF VODOUN

Vodoun is not only a religion but a body of beliefs and practices applied chiefly but not exclusively by the Haitian peasantry in their efforts to survive in their environment. "Sad Tropics," said French anthropologist Claude Lévi-Strauss.[3] This verdict and a low level of technological knowledge explain the predominance of Vodoun in the Haitian way of life. The peasant whose knowledge of science is limited must rely on the available interpretation of the environment and this is mainly a supernaturalistic one.[4] Crop failures, pests, droughts, and floods are not interpreted as natural phenomena but as manifestations of the anger of neglected spirits or the envy of some neighbor. Equally, success is attributed to the protection of the gods or the magical power of an individual. In the valley of Marbial in 1948, most peasants were convinced that with enough money one could "buy" rain and have it fall on one's plot. Sickness and its sequel, death, are seldom thought to be due to natural causes. Souls are stolen and kept in bottles; illnesses are "sent"; magic turns the most healthy man sexually impotent; the blood of babies is sucked at a distance; tuberculosis can be cured by transferring it to a rooster. Proper offerings can secure success in economic, political, and amorous ventures. Since "an ounce of prevention is worth a pound of cure," preventive and counter-magic are available in the form of amulets, "points," special garments and the like.

We would not say that the Haitian peasant lives in a world of "fear and trembling," but we believe that his limited ability to interpret natural phenomena leaves him no other course than to rely heavily on magical practices. But, one may say, magic is not Vodoun. Academically speaking this may be so. In reality, both bodies of belief are so closely interrelated as to constitute only one complex: the magico-religious. For more than 160 years that complex has been the mainstay of Haitian country life. If we have emphasized its magical aspect so far, it is only to underline its weakness and to make clear that we do not consider the magico-religious complex the best of solutions. That an alternative did exist is made evident by the early efforts of Haitian leadership, even prior to 1804, to create institutions and associations capable of giving the country an orientation towards *natural* behavior. However, the isolation that we have described was incompatible with Europeanization. When this isolation is added to the scarcity of resources, the corruption and the incompetence, it becomes clear why Haiti failed to extend to its masses adequate hygiene, education, and technology. Yet, the extent to which the country did survive is due to the relative success of the peasantry in organizing itself without the assistance of the educated urban element and in some instances even *in spite of* that element.

For example, in the field of group relations, a cooperative labor system was formed to accomplish agricultural tasks. Such *sociétés* as they were called, became obsolete with the atomization of rural property. The rural family, under the stern guidance of its eldest member, became a fairly efficient social unit dominated by the spirit of mutual help. The Haitian peasant, like his counterparts elsewhere, was not an enthusiastic innovator or inventor in the field of agriculture. He used some African and colonial techniques but he forgot others. He did not prune his coffee trees, nor did he use fertilizers or systematic crop rotation. He used his limited agricultural skill to good advantage in the volcanic soil and his coffee crop has been the chief source of income to the country since its independence. Today, soil exhaustion, erosion, and demographic pressure call for radical changes in the field of agricultural techniques.

Vodoun is the main achievement of rural Haiti. The conspiratorial cult of colonial times grew and adapted itself to the multiple needs of an isolated agricultural society, offering solutions to its problems, providing it with entertainment and the means to compensate the harshness of daily life. Some of its aspects are dreadful, but its versatility and its positive role are well expressed by Jahn[5] in his quite accurate definition of the *hounfor* or temple as "Sanctuary, clubhouse, dance hall, hospital, theatre, chemist's shop, music hall, court and council chamber in one." Furthermore, the magico-religious complex can be considered as a moderator of violence. At least prior to 1957, murders were a rare occurrence in the Haitian countryside and the few cases that were registered were usually associated with disputes over land ownership. The explanation might be that the Haitian considers magic to be a more sensible weapon to use against his enemy than one which risks jail. The psychological results can be quite satisfactory if the victim comes to suspect that he is bewitched, a conclusion that he will reach only too easily with the help of the magician. As can be seen, however, the moderating effect in turn creates a chain reaction of countermagic which threatens the cohesion of the community and even of the family. *Houngans* and *bocors* live by keeping their clientele on a constant alert and by sustaining belief in the supernatural interpretation of the environment. Should the peasantry, the urban proletariat, and a sector of the bourgeoisie lose their faith in the capacity of the Vodoun clergy to manipulate nature and its phenomena at will, *houngans* and *bocors*[6] would face a serious loss of income and social power. But that loss of faith can come only when education, sanitation, and improved economic conditions alleviate the chronic insecurity. Such a program is well beyond the national resources, both financial and human, of Haiti. As long as these improvements are not introduced, Vodoun will reign supreme over goods and lives. It will operate beyond class lines since it offers to some members of the educated minority a last hope against illnesses which the professional physician cannot cure. As long as insecurity prevails, urbanites and peasants will seek from the *houngan* the secret of wealth and the key to political and social advancement.

Thus, it is hard to see Vodoun in perspective. It unites and divides, cures and kills, protects and persecutes all at once. More than the state it has succeeded in giving to the Haitian masses a sense of belonging. Perhaps more successfully than Creole as a unifying language, Vodoun has erased the tribal differences among the former slaves of the French colony by imposing coexistence on their divers gods. To be sure, traces of tribalism do survive. The Nago rite may be predominant in the north, the Ibo in the south-west, the Congo in the valley of Jacmel, but in some places all their *loas*, with the exception of the dreaded Pétros, dwell peacefully in the same *hounfor*.[7] Yet when all has been said, good and bad, one condemning aspect of Vodoun remains. Historically the religion, like all religions, has evolved and then suffered a process of stagnation which is fatal to the interest of Haiti. It undoubtedly possesses a certain dynamism and undergoes super-ficial changes.[8] But it has lost its original revolutionary impetus. It has turned into a conservative institution which condones and feeds upon the back-wardness of the peasantry. Moreover, Vodoun lacks a hierarchy capable of formulating and imposing a new policy for the benefit of the rural popula-tion. It can only thwart or at least remain indifferent to the efforts of the state to initiate changes which might menace the local control of the *houngans* over their flocks. To our knowledge, no *houngan* has ever sponsored the building of a school, promoted a program of community development, sought to introduce new crops, or innovated an agricultural technique. His overspecialization not only guarantees him relative power and wealth, but it also makes him unfit for the kind of *true* leadership which places the material and spiritual welfare of the community above personal advantages. The type of change needed today is beyond the comprehension of Vodoun and contrary to its interests.

Vodoun will remain the bane of Haiti and the arch-enemy of the progressive state until its clergy is curbed by a superior power and learns to cooperate with the rural teacher, the physician, and the agronomist. But should this metamorphosis occur, the *houngan* would cease to be *houngan;* he would turn into a civil servant. The gods would die.

POLITICS, POLITICIANS, AND VODOUN

That Vodoun played an important role in the politics of colonial Haiti has been demonstrated. However, its experience since the dawn of independence has varied from open hostility, to tolerance and official support.

It may seem strange that none of Haiti's three foremost Black heroes, Toussaint L'Ouverture, Dessalines, and Christophe, had any open sympathy for Vodoun. L'Ouverture's abhorrence for the cult has been attributed to his sincere Catholicism. We think differently. A politician of his stature who, like many politicians, used cunning and deceit when they suited his purpose, would have had no qualms about practicing Vodoun if his plans could have benefited from such a compromise. L'Ouverture knew only too well what he wanted and in addition, he "knew his friends and his enemies even better." The cult of African origin was among the latter. The man was proud of his race, but he believed that the African cultural heritage had no place in the Americas. Independence, economic prosperity, and political stability could be achieved only through a thorough Europeanization of Haiti. He was a true *créole* in that sense, a slave born in the New World, acculturated to French values and disdainful of African behavior. The imposition of Catholicism, centralized power, and strict control of the free labor force on the plantations were the three capital elements of his policy. Vodoun with its capacity to sway the masses, its secrecy and conspiratorial nature, was a challenge to the state that L'Ouverture could not tolerate. Quite often while fighting the British invader or the French, he had to divert some of his forces to destroy bands of dissidents led by Vodoun priests.

Vodoun did have a *revolutionary* path of action: the total break-up of the colonial system. L'Ouverture's aim was *evolutionary:* to modify that same structure for the benefit of the country. He meant to keep the white settlers, to maintain the large estates whose production would be equally divided among state, owner, and workers, and to promote commerce with the United States, not to isolate the community.

L'Ouverture's successor, Dessalines, was victorious on the battlefield but lacking in administrative skill. Nevertheless, he was even harsher on Vodounists and although he tried to foster Catholicism officially, it was of little personal concern to him. His anti-Vodoun policies arose from a similar need to eliminate foci of opposition to his authority.

Dessalines was murdered in 1806 after a short rule. He was forgiven by his victims, for ironically enough, he became a *loa*, a god of the Vodoun pantheon. The religion he persecuted honors him as the Emperor; his downfall is a warning to Haitian leaders of the consequences when the African spirits are neglected.

Henri Christophe, king of northern Haiti until his suicide in 1820, favored both Catholicism and Protestantism. His supposedly secret addiction to Vodoun belongs more to the domain of legend and novel than to history.

Our emphasis on the early period of Haiti's development is to make clear two facts: (1) Vodoun was considered to be a political force at an early time. But the conflict of goals between Vodoun and national policy meant that the former had to be crushed if the latter were to be successful. (2) Catholicism was seen as a necessary instrument of evolution since its clergy could be persuaded to operate along the lines of national policy. The double failure of L'Ouverture and Christophe signified the triumph of Vodoun. From then on, no head of state had the same opportunity, resources, personality, or energy to launch a movement of national proportions to stamp out this apparent obstacle to the Europeanization of Haiti. Rather, the balance of power changed and rulers began to compromise with Vodoun instead of repressing it.

One exception may be President Riché, the old general who ruled Haiti for a period in the 1840's and whose distaste for Vodoun verged on the pathological. When awakened in the dead of night by the sound of distant drums, he would get dressed, march to the sound of the hated instruments, and fall upon the believers, beating them mercilessly with his heavy stick.

Shortly after the rule of the old general, General Faustin Soulouque was elected President. He was the choice of the mulattos who saw in him an inoffensive and docile puppet. This was a bitter mistake. Soulouque was quick to display a stubbornness, courage, pride, and lust for power that dealt a severe blow to the hold of the mulattos on internal politics. He held two more cards that favored his winning solid popular support: intransigent nationalism and the nearly open practice of Vodoun. We can see in him a distant forerunner of François Duvalier.

During Soulouque's tenure of office (1847-1859), the French were incensed by the mistreatment of some nationals at the hands of the Haitian police and chose to use "gunboat diplomacy." They dispatched a naval squadron to Port-au-Prince. Admiral Duquesne demanded an indemnity and threatened to bombard the capital. Soulouque was not impressed and the admiral had to use softer language.

It is possible that Soulouque believed in Vodoun but he certainly made no bones about practicing it, if we can believe the reports that he organized ceremonies at the National Palace. When traveling, he saw no shame whatsoever in abandoning his escort at the sound of the drums and going to pay his respects to the *loas*. Although Soulouque was nearly illiterate and unable to benefit from sociological theories, he was the first to reap political benefits from the mixture of nationalism, class struggle, and Vodoun. He was not only a tyrant and a cruel man, but a shrewd politician as well. In order to enhance his prestige with the masses and perhaps out of personal ambition and vanity, Soulouque revived the title taken by Dessalines and turned himself into Emperor Faustin I. Vodounist or not, he insisted upon having a Catholic priest officiate at the coronation.

Haiti then became the subject of pitiless mockery in the foreign press. The French in particular took advantage of the situation to ridicule indirectly another emperor, Napoleon III, the president who also chose (but after Soulouque) to play upon popular imagination by imitating his great-uncle. Soulouque's abuses and his costly and useless military campaigns against the Dominican Republic, which he sought to return to Haitian rule,[9] caused disaffection among his supporters. He was easily ousted by the mulatto general Geffrard, the man who signed the concordat with the Vatican.

Vodoun continued to figure in Haitian life, but its role in politics suffered an eclipse when its status between 1860 and 1900 is compared with the favor it enjoyed under Emperor Faustin. We can only surmise its presence from tales of local chieftains who enjoyed the reputation of being bulletproof or of possessing the gift of ubiquity due to their Vodoun power. Undoubtedly some uprisings of ambitious generals were preceded by ceremonies aimed at impressing their troops of usually illiterate and magic-minded peasants.

Thus it becomes clear why Vodoun enjoyed the protection of the authorities. It had become an indispensable ingredient of the political cuisine. A chief who was not credited with supernatural power was lacking "something." Worse, if he neglected Vodoun, he was depriving himself of a sure source of intelligence, since his opponents eventually would have to court some prestigious *houngan* when the time for a coup came. If the *houngan* was on the side of the authorities, he would play informant. The important fact is not whether these warlords believed in Vodoun and its efficacy. The crux of the matter is that in order to play the game of real-politik they could not ignore the usefulness of Vodoun as a means of control and prestige.

Vodoun, however, does not have the kind of hierarchical structure that can be manipulated. Degrees of initiation leading to "hounganhood" exist, but each priest rules over his own temple and assistants. If he is believed to enjoy the favors of especially powerful spirits, if he has a strong personality and exceptional skill, he will gain fame and even something like nationwide prestige. But such prominence does not entitle him to dominate his colleagues institutionally. Such lack of hierarchy also excludes joint action among *houngans* and fosters open rivalry among them. Moreover, regionalism creates local interests and attachment to local leaders. Thus a president from the North might well align the provisional loyalty of the *houngans* of his area, but what about the others in the South and West or the Artibonite? A master politician's dream would be to accumulate so much power and create so much fear about his person as to be able to impose himself upon the whole Vodoun clergy.

Few executives of Haiti, with the possible exception of Soulouque, really tried to carry out such a scheme, until Dr. Duvalier appeared. One other president, Antoine Simon, a former rural policeman from the South, did show such impulses. Between 1906 and 1911 the National Palace once more became sacred ground for Vodoun activities, but we cannot be sure whether Simon was led by the *houngans* or whether he dominated them. His own daughter was reputed to be a priestess and has even been credited with performing a human sacrifice. Such an exaggeration probably was due to the malice of the bourgeoisie whose constant derision of the president provoked him to harass them with childish vexations. The hapless Simon, who involved himself in a petty financial scandal over bananas and railroads, was toppled by a general from the North, this time a member of a well-to-do family.

General Leconte was the last of the few energetic and capable presidents of Haiti before disaster struck. He presumably was blown up with the National Palace in 1912. His death was followed by a period of political chaos which forced upon Haitian pride and nationalism the unsavory attention of the United States; in July 1915, Admiral Capperton ordered the Marines ashore.

There was resistance, but it was doomed to fail. The stubborn little country whose numerous constitutions for over a century had defiantly denied the right of property to foreigners (that is, whites) was bankrupt, both morally and materially. In northern and central Haiti guerrilla fighting broke out when the Occupation forces with excessive harshness began imposing the *corvée* on the ruralite. This method of obligatory and unpaid labor had been long abandoned by Haitian authorities. Under improvised but gallant leadership the peasant war lasted until 1921. Vodoun did not openly participate in it; no *houngan* rose against the invader, no messianic movement took form to announce the salvation of people and country. The *houngans* were content to sell amulets to the faithful for protection against bullets. Vodoun in 1915 was not what it had been in 1791.

Many justifications of the Occupation were offered: insolvency and anarchy were put forth together with the absurd excuse that it was a preventive measure against Germany's intention to take over Haiti. Germany was at war and blockaded. It would be nearer to the truth to say that American capital expected to exploit Haiti and turn it into another Cuba or Puerto Rico. But the hopes of American businessmen were short-lived. Defeated in battle, the peasantry won on a grander field. Their passive resistance proved its efficacy once more. Of the large-scale agricultural ventures launched in Haiti, only two, a sugar factory and a sisal plantation, survived the Occupation (1915-1934).

Let us consider the influence of the American intervention upon Haitian politics and Vodoun. After peace was restored, roads, schools, and dispensaries were built and programs of agricultural extension were launched. Vodoun was prohibited not so much on political grounds but as a manifestation of backwardness and magic. The drums were silent for a time or were beaten only after the authorities had granted permission to organize a "dance." But Vodoun flourished simply because stability and a certain degree of prosperity meant that funds were available for ceremonies of thanks to the loas. The symbiotic relation between Vodoun and business has been drawn by the Haitian writer Milo Rigaud.[10] According to him, business blossoms when religion does because many kinds of goods must be bought for the ritual. We believe the reverse to be true. Economic welfare, high prices for coffee, and peace activate Vodoun because the peasants, as we have just stated, grasp the opportunity to perform long-standing and costly obligations to the protective spirits. Moreover, in times of plenty Vodoun takes on a festive mood and its magical aspect recedes to the extent that security and good health increase.

Outwardly, the American Occupation seemed on the way toward achieving the westernization (the "Progress" of the previous century) which had been the dream of so many Haitian heads of state. Material advances were patent, administrative efficiency satisfactory, credit and solvency good. The armed forces, reduced in size and turned into a constabulary, were apparently cured of their chronic illness: political fever. The presidents, chosen from the educated mulatto elite, remained true patriots even when they agreed to collaborate with the Occupation forces. They did their best to preserve the basic rights of their country. If they showed a discreet interest in Vodoun as popular songs and spurious anecdotes tend to make us believe, it was in terms of a concession to reality, a kind of political investment made with the hope of "increasing return." This return might be the support of a powerful houngan or some measure of popularity if the presidents could convey the idea that at heart they still felt sympathy for the spirits while political necessity forced them to demonstrate condescension or hostility.

Sudre Dartiguenave (1915-1922), affectionately known as "Cathead," fought American pressure with the classic weapon of the weaker opponent: astuteness. His successor, the lawyer Louis Borno (1922-1930), author of correct if not inspired poems about the Holy Virgin, had an easier task at first: peasant guerrilla fighting had ceased and a loan of forty million dollars enabled his government to undertake an impressive and practical program of public works.

However, new forces eventually turned the tables on Borno and ultimately erased most of the benefits Haiti had drawn from the bitter humiliation of the Occupation. National disaster usually calls for a reappraisal of the socio-cultural values which failed to avert it. The past is put in the dock and found guilty without appeal. In the Haiti of 1928 the trial took an unexpected turn: The country was in misery because its responsible elite had rejected its intrinsic personality, trying to be what they were not, European instead of African. By concatenation this original sin had caused a split in the Haitian social body, turning the responsible class away from its duties towards the rural masses and transforming it into a parasitic, superficial, and prejudiced clique. It had debased the real national values by piling up mockery and contempt upon the peasantry, its way of life and its ancestral beliefs. Only by returning to its cultural sources could Haiti regenerate itself and regain its pride.

The authors of such criticism belong to two distinct social classes and ideologies. On one side were what we may call the Young Turks, scions of wealthy bourgeois families, educated abroad and imbued with Marxist theories. On the other side were a mature physician and civil servant, Dr. Jean Price-Mars and, later, his disciples, young Black intellectuals to whom the democratizing effect of the American Occupation upon education had given freer access to higher learning and the liberal professions. Both sides had a common motivation — nationalism — and a common aim — end the Occupation. The Young Turks engaged in political agitation and organized the strikes and street fighting which brought about the collapse of President Borno's regime in 1930. Four years later the Marines withdrew, leaving Haiti the master of its fate. Success spelled the doom of the Young Turks. Most of them succumbed to the lure of plush jobs in the corrupt and dictatorial government of Sténio Vincent (1930-1941). A few recalcitrant ones were jailed, beaten, and advised to go into exile. However, the leftist movement did recover from the blow.

What about Price-Mars and his young Black disciples? They continued studying folklore, talking about folklore, and writing about folklore, but they were only biding their time. Vodoun became the central topic of folklore; it became so acceptable as to become a bore. So the institution which had been banned by the Occupation forces and the regimes fostered by them returned in triumph. This did not mean that Vodoun was practiced openly. The triumph consisted in its rehabilitation as something authentically Haitian. Its authenticity sprang from its association with the peasantry, "the real country." The peasants were Blacks, so an authentic Haiti should be ruled by the Blacks, the "Authentics." The proposition was quite legitimate. Why should a minority of Black and mulatto bourgeois live off the fat of the land without benefits for the masses? President Elie Lescot (1941-1946), who ineptly favored ill-qualified light-skinned citizens over educated Blacks for government posts, offered the Authentics the occasion they were waiting for.[11] Although the revolution which overthrew Lescot had a strong leftist inspiration, it was the Blacks who profited from it. As usual, the leftists were tamed by offers of some juicy appointments while the incorruptible ones were murdered by the regime of President Estimé (1946-1950), an "improvement" over the methods of Vincent.

Black bourgoisie, spectacular spending, class struggle, tourism and Vodoun for tourists marked the passage of Estimé as President of Haiti. An opportunity to make some lasting changes in the economic structure of the Republic was lost through lack of planning and true revolutionary spirit. In spite of his popularity, Estimé was forced by the Army to retire, providing a lesson his Minister of Health, Dr. François Duvalier, did not forget.

The new chief of state, General (then Colonel) Magloire undertook to lessen the class struggle. He also built roads, a costly dam, and some housing projects, and appeared on the cover of *Time* magazine. But turning dictatorial and allowing too much corruption, Magloire was sent to exile with surprising ease by a general strike in December 1956. By a strange coincidence, this period of Latin American history witnessed the fall of many military regimes and the establishment of democratic ones — until the time when international necessity recalled the strongmen.

In 1957 it was the opinion of the United States Department of State that Haiti needed a middle-class, middle-of-the-road reformer. Of the four candidates for the presidency, only one met the requirements. He was the mild mannered, almost naive physician who had devoted years to curing peasants of yaws and had spent his moments of leisure studying Vodoun. Dr. François Duvalier seemed the perfect choice. He was elected by popular vote and the blessing of the Army on a date he had personally chosen: September 22, 1957. The date was a sinister warning. On September 22, 1882, President Lysius Salomon, a Black general well versed in economics and wearied by the provocations of the mulattos, had loosed the mob of Port-au-Prince against them. The looting, burning, and killing lasted three days.

4 DUVALIER AND VODOUN

The relationship between Duvalier and Vodoun should be viewed not as one of an individual to a faith, but rather it should be approached from the standpoint of the relations between church and state. For *raison d'État* not a few heads of state will participate in religious ceremonies although they may be agnostics or downright atheists. This is considered to be sounc policy. In his *Mémoires* Saint-Simon relates with a touch of bitterness how he vainly prompted the Duke of Orléans, then Regent of France, to show himself at the processions and other celebrations of the Catholic Church in order to gain popular sympathy and confidence for his government. The Regent adamantly declined to perform such a boring duty. He was a poor politician.

Few Haitians, holders or candidates to an elective office, will display such a lack of common sense. They will cultivate the friendship of the key *houngans* of their district, make donations to their temples, offer ceremonies and, in addition, go to Mass every Sunday. They become vulnerable to black-mail on the part of their "friends," but this is the price they must pay for the support and the favorable influence the *houngans* will exercise upon the electorate.

The relations between state and church are a trial of strength, a con-flict of interests. In Haiti, as elsewhere, the theory that the state holds "the monopoly of legitimate physical force"[12] is seriously weakened by the ex-istence of groups and institutions wielding other types of forces: economic, social, and religious. The complex interactions of such forces against the state are at the roots of the rise of Vodoun in Haiti since 1957, though Vo-doun itself represented a power which more than once had undermined the state. Haiti has too few permanent institutions upon which a government can hope to rest. There are no political parties: there is no continuity in the public service, no "loyal opposition." By 1937, three years after the end of the American Occupation, the Army once more became ill with political fever.

Power then is personal; the state becomes *one* man: the executive, who with little pain can dispose of independent senators and congressmen as if they were caddies. The meager financial resources must be spent on creating supernumerary jobs for partisans, informants, and parasites. A president lasts as long as he can manage to keep the opposition divided, and the opposition is the whole conscious population minus one citizen—the president.

The situation confronting Duvalier in 1957 was not far different from this somewhat pessimistic picture. To be sure, the Army had backed him, but who could trust the Army? The Catholic clergy and the bourgeoisie were openly predicting his fall and flight within a few months. A large sector of the Black intelligentsia was resolutely against him. The rural areas were divided in loyalty and its masses in expectancy. The majority of the businessmen did not trust him, although those who had financed his campaign did hope he would last long enough for them to recover their money or receive compensatory advantages. The United States Department of State and the Episcopal Church were sympathetic, but how long would their interests coincide with the plans and ambitions of Duvalier?

In 1966, nine years later, François Duvalier is sole master of Haiti. By using naked force, murder, cunning, temerity, blackmail, nationalism, and Vodoun he has crushed the Opposition, cowed the Catholic Church, outsmarted the United States Department of State, rendered the Army impotent, and bled business white. If the capacity to remain in power were the sole yardstick by which to measure the skill of a politician, we could say that Duvalier is a success. But his success would mean only the triumph of one man and the rout of a nation. The plight of Haiti is too well known to dwell on it; suffice it to say that many publicists consider today's Haiti as "the poorest country on earth." Nor is it far from the truth to view the tiny Black Republic as being in full regression. However, our concern is for Vodoun, and we cannot understand its resurgency in Haiti properly without setting it in the general political context.

We can safely consider the tenure of office of Duvalier, so far, as a ceaseless struggle against all kinds of foes, and in all fairness some of the negative character of his government can be laid at the door of that bitter opposition. Any other man would have chosen to retire, but stubbornness, tenacity of purpose, and in a sense, the response to the challenge brought the former rural physician to seek and follow the path of absolute power regardless of the cost in suffering and frustration to his fellow citizens. He used the weapons available. To his cause he enlisted all possible allies in defiance of international opinion and with total disregard for future consequences. He has succeeded in building a formidable machine of oppressive control which he, even as a master sorcerer, may now be unable to steer towards constructive action.

Duvalier's battle against the opposition has been fought on simultaneous and connected fronts, but we will emphasize only the one action which is most closely connected with our topic and which sheds light on his whole strategy and its relation to Vodoun. We will discuss the struggle between the state and the churches; we purposefully write *churches* because Catholicism, Vodoun, and Protestantism were parties or victims in the encounter.

A few words about the respective relations of the three creeds with the body social are necessary for a better understanding of the operations. Catholicism is the dominant faith, but its ability to control suffers from a number of limitations. Its principal ally, the mulatto and Black bourgeoisie, is not strong enough to win a favorable decision by itself; it needs the support or, at least, the indifference of the Army.

The peasant practices both Catholicism and Vodoun with hardly a pang of conscience. But the Haitian ruralite is not a religious fanatic; he is tolerant and generally feels no deep attachment to the curate. He fears the civilian authorities, "the State," more than the priests, and he fears the *houngan* even more than the authorities.

The Catholic clergy of Haiti is not united; it is still two-thirds white, while the native third is itself divided between the ever present factions: Blacks and mulattos. The bishoprics and key positions are held by foreigners at a time when nationalism and anti-colonialism are on the rise. Add to these factors the ambition, legitimate or not, of some Haitian prelates and the weakness of the Catholic clergy becomes patent.

Protestantism is not only numerically feeble (involving 10% of the people, it is said), but the presence of various denominations — Baptist, Adventist, Wesleyan — precludes all joint action. The Episcopal Church is fairly strong because of its financial resources, but it can do little more than make its voice heard. Finally, there is Vodoun, the most formidable adversary of the state.

Let us remember that until Duvalier had dealt with that source of nuisance, the Army, he could not stay in power. Lacking in esprit-de-corps and divided into political factions, the rank and file as well as the officer corps were easily purged of suspicious elements.[13] Once the Army had been made toothless by concentrating weapons in the hands of the well-known *Tonton Macoutes* and later the militia, the gradual liquidation of the other sources of opposition was a question of time and opportunity. Duvalier did not provoke them openly; quite the contrary. For the first time, I believe, in the country's history, he appointed a Haitian prelate as Minister of Education. Although this move may have been inspired by respect, it could well have been calculated to mark the beginning of a promising era for the native clergy. In a way, it was a sort of message: "Here is the proof of my nationalism. Rally to my government and reap ecclesiastical promotions." On the other hand, to demonstrate his independence from Catholicism, Duvalier openly courted the Episcopal Church which had given him its blessing jointly with the United States Department of State during the presidential campaign. So far, all was in order.

Although the higher Catholic clergy must have been aware of its own weakness, it chose to show its displeasure with the behavior of the executive. On moral grounds it could not remain silent in front of the increasing wave of murders, abuses, and practice of Vodoun. After preliminary skirmishes during which the Catholic press was muzzled, the final stroke was as swift as it was unexpected: the Archbishop of Port-au-Prince, two bishops, and a number of influential French priests were summarily ejected in quick succession from the country. Shortly afterwards, the head of the Episcopal Church suffered a similar fate: He "was arrested and expelled at gun point on a half hour's notice."[14] The Papal Nuncio was recalled and Duvalier was excommunicated. But this did not impede another Haitian prelate from keeping the Portfolio of Education. He had succumbed evidently to the double call of nationalism and ambition.

What do the men in the street and the peasants think of a president who deals such defiant blows? What is the opinion of a president who stands up to the United States, triumphs over repeated invasions, escapes from attempted assassination, and crushes plots before they hatch? The answers are multiple, but all reveal admiration, grudging or not, and chiefly awe: "He is not afraid of the white man.[15] He is strong, he has *power*, magical power, the *loas* are on his side!" Not in vain did Duvalier woo Vodoun during the twenty years prior to his election. As president, he has openly espoused the popular religion, but we must consider his action a *mariage de raison* and not one of love. Dr. François Duvalier may not be a great scholar, but his long contacts with Haitian life taught him some essential truths: the westernization of Haiti was only superficial. The great masses were still in the grip of the magico-religious way of thought. Since Duvalier must have read Lévy-Bruhl,[16] he may have regarded the mentality of his fellow countrymen as "primitive" and "pre-logical." The real focus of power, the rural masses, had not been exploited by the heads of state, save during the War of Independence. An effectively controlled peasantry could well outweigh the urban minority, including business and the Army. Vodoun was foremost among the tools required to carry out that scheme for absolute power.

Two presidents had reached the same conclusions instinctively, but Soulouque and Simon failed because they *believed* in Vodoun. Their faith easily rendered them the tools of the *houngans;* they were not the masters of their political decisions. Not so with Duvalier! Only if he does *not* believe can he expect to impose his will on his reluctant collaborators. His will is supported by his pretense of conformity, and by the repeated "proofs" that he possesses magical powers to a superlative degree. In the event that his magical prestige does not suffice, he holds a trump card: armed force. As early as 1958 some prominent *houngans* met an untimely death; we do not know whether more of their kind failed to heed the notice that they had a new master.

To deal with Catholicism and Protestantism was child's play. Their futile attempt to bar the road to absolutism required only one blow: "Strike the shepherd and the flock scatters." Vodoun is made of harder stuff, it has a thousand heads, its "bishops" are legion, and this makes the struggle between the state and that particular church only fiercer. It might be enough to disorganize Protestantism momentarily and to divide and confuse the Catholic clergy. The danger of a Catholic schism headed by native elements might demand extra caution in the dealings with the Vatican. But Vodoun had no external support. It had to be dealt with thoroughly and reduced to total obeisance. The moment was propitious for the state.

Until a decade or so ago it was not unusual for Haitian peasants to believe that Nord Alexis, the octogenarian general who ruled early in this century, was *still* president; the more educated spoke of Borno (1922-1930) as "sitting in the Palace." Such times are gone. The presence of Duvalier is not only known but felt in the remotest corners of Haiti. All *houngans* and *bocors* must acknowledge the existence of a superior authority within their own sphere of influence.

This is the real revolution of Duvalier: His armed militia is everywhere, but its chiefs hold only crumbs of power. None of them so far can hope to extend his control beyond a narrow territory. Recruited from the peasantry, the urban proletariat, and the expanding lower middle class, many militiamen and *macoutes* believe and practice Vodoun. Undoubtedly some of them belong to the Vodoun clergy. In them, politics have been amalgamated with religious faith and loyalty to a leader. This has created fanaticism, an attitude so uncommon in Haiti. The excessive zeal of the militia is directed toward one man, Duvalier, who derives from it both political and religious strength. The *houngans* of yesterday have consequently lost the control they long exercised upon their community. If they still hold some power it is for services rendered to the state or because they are willing to serve it. The triumph of Vodoun demands the submission of its clergy. The once independent religion is in chains. In a way it is the spouse of the state and performs her duties at command.

Although the economic debacle of Haiti and heavy taxes hinder the practice of Vodoun, ceremonies are organized, the drums beat and people dance, but the ritual is under government control. The government orders it and pays for it. Duvalier does not love Vodoun, he only uses it. To what purpose?

Clergymen, educated Haitians, foreigners, all miss the point when they try to denigrate Duvalier by accusing him of "voodooism." The attacks only enhance his stature among the masses and confirm his nationalism among his followers. His brand of nationalism is a special one that dictates a policy not guided by national interests but vitiated by ideological and doctrinal prejudices, precisely opposed to what a national policy should be.

But Duvalier cares little if the people are hungry, diseased, and illiterate. Perhaps he despises the Haitian people. He is that rare blend of dreamer and man of action who is fascinated by a theory which he holds to be the absolute truth. Haiti is Black and must be ruled by Blacks. Further, its ethnic cohesion must be strengthened by a religious symbol of its own, Vodoun. Haiti must have a National Faith and a national faith calls for a national head of the church: Duvalier. The idea is not a novel one if we remember Henry VIII of England or, without going back so far, Nazism.[17] If our thesis seems too far fetched, let us analyze a project of Duvalier. Late in 1957 he decided to change the Haitian flag from blue and red horizontal to black and red vertical, the black to the staff. Instead of the coat-of-arms designed by the mulatto president, Alexandre Pétion, Duvalier proposed that a guineafowl perched on a conch (the *lambi* which called the slaves to rebellion) was to stand at the upper left corner (dexter chief point). His proposal was greeted by a volley of protests, and since he had been in power only a few months, he withdrew his plans. It was said that the operation would be too costly. But in June 1964, the flag *was* changed; the full version with bird and shell going to the Army and a bastard one, keeping the old coat-of-arms, flying upon public buildings and embassies.

Historically there exists some doubts about the original colors of the flag; it might have been black and red. However, the blue and red horizontal was a symbol of national unity: Blacks and mulattos were supposedly equal, both sharing in state affairs (the staff). When the red is out on the black and red vertical flag it means that the Blacks are solely in control and the class struggle is won. But the bird signifies constant vigilance and the conch represents the call to massacre. There can be no clearer warning.

Lastly, in 1918, an esotericist of sorts, Arthur Holly, wrote a turgid book, *Les Daimons du culte voudo,* in which he advanced the thesis that the position of the colors of the national flag were in flagrant opposition to the esoteric forces. In order for Haiti to progress they should be set vertically. Dr. Duvalier probably smiles at such nonsense, but at the same time his decision to modify the flag expresses recognition of a political and social symbol. It gains him extra dividends: *houngans* and fanatic followers will have one more reason to believe in his wisdom and occult knowledge.

A president dressed in white tie is a common sight. It better suits the head of a national church to don more impressive trappings and to hold a more exclusive title. The title of Emperor is well associated with Vodoun. If Duvalier did wish to be crowned "Emperor," as it seems, it was not to satisfy his personal vanity, but for strictly political reasons. For the believers, he would have become equal to Dessalines, although for the bourgeoisie and the foreigners he would have been only a new Soulouque.

But whether Haiti under Duvalier ever becomes an Empire for the third time or not, her history will have gone full circle back to 1804, but with a qualitative difference. At the start of her independent life she was considered "out of place" because she had won her freedom against all expectations. The temporary isolation sought by her founder was motivated by the existence of real enemies; the subsequent failure of the responsible class confirmed that isolation. Today, Haiti is an anachronism, not because of a possible change in the form of government, but on account of a policy which condemns her people to live *en vase clos,* imposing on the peasants in the name of nationalism, the continuity of the very way of life which has denied them the benefits of health and education. By a cruel irony, a sector of the learned minority is responsible for the regression, this time not through failure to act but by deliberate choice. Here is a perfect example of what Julien Benda labeled *la trahison des clercs,* the treason of the learned. The honest attempt at rehabilitating Vodoun by searching for the truth about it was corrupted by selfish and narrow class interests and became a political nightmare. The Haitian *clercs* mistook their passionate interest in folklore for the active care they should have taken of their illiterate brothers. Folklore is beneficial to a country when it keeps esthetic values alive and is a mark of originality. But when it becomes the essence of a nation's behavior as it has in Haiti today, it can only obscure the prospects for positive change.

REACTION TO VODOUN

Though it is in bonds and under state control, Vodoun is at the height of its career. Its triumph over a century of Catholic opposition and over generation after generation of inimical Haitian writers, politicians, and scholars, however, is not due to its own dynamism. It is due, rather, to its powerful associations with politics, nationalism, and the class struggle. All during the long feud, Vodoun had the majority on its side, but until 1964, that majority had little of the organized leadership which the opposition supposedly had. The story of the reaction to Vodoun is fraught with conformism, futility, irresponsibility, intolerance, and few instances of clear-sightedness. In a word, an all too human episode.

During the last third of the nineteenth century and the first two decades of the twentieth, the Haitian intellectuals who took positions against the "primitive rituals" of the peasants did so for two reasons: (1) To defend their country from unfair and at times vicious attacks from abroad. Their patriotism conformed to the dominant European attitude of the period which considered everything non-white to be inferior. They had to lie piously about Vodoun by pretending that much of its reputed power over the masses was false or exaggerated. (2) To distinguish themselves from the ignorant peasantry, both Blacks and mulattos decried the barbaric practices. Those who had been educated in Europe, who were sincere Catholics, who spoke good French and knew their classics as well as any, were the true Haiti. This was a futile and cowardly defense.

From these two categories of *clercs* there were only a few who transformed their opposition to Vodoun into practical measures when they entered the field of politics. A couple of Ministers of Education tackled the problem the right way by launching programs of integral rural education. But their very initiative was their undoing. Men of such energy could aspire only to the presidency, so their career was usually brief. Illiterate generals do not trust intellectuals.

The surge of Negro culture in the nineteen twenties, the spread of jazz, the emergence of poets and novelists, the interest of white societies in the exotic and the unspoiled, the very movement which, in combination with nationalism, started the reappraisal of Vodoun in Haiti, did not disarm the adversaries of the African side of Haitian culture. In the name of Catholicism and of their French heritage, they repeatedly scored the demoralizing effect of Vodoun, associating it with backwardness and maintaining that all *houngans* were rogues.

The novel was the favorite form for such attacks. With little risk to the authors it could display sharp criticisms of the frequent associations of politicians and their wives with Vodoun. In order to drive the lesson home, the wives are usually seduced by the *houngans*. All very trite. These writers had more concern for the morality and proper behavior of the bourgeoisie than for the welfare of the rural and urban proletariat. A later group of novelists, belonging to a younger generation, are moderate in their criticism of Vodoun. They exploit it as a literary asset, but they emphasize the social change occurring among the peasants in order to predict the gradual disappearance of the religion.

In sum, the intellectuals on the side of Vodoun have been, for better or worse, more efficient than their opponents. Their task has been easier since with little critical sense they were also obeying the password given once more from abroad: Exalt your African heritage. In Africa, itself, the *clercs* have known how far to go. In Haiti the brakes failed.

If there is little wonder that individuals acting by the pen and without a program should have failed to dent the structure and power of Vodoun, it is astounding that an institution which is intrinsically committed to oppose a "pagan" religion should have made so little progress in the battle. Although the Catholic Church was poorly represented during the colonial period and the first sixty years of Haiti's independent life, its troubles were more basic. In the very beginning it adopted an inappropriate type of administration and its apostolic action lacked dynamism. While its clergy was ill-prepared to cope with "heathens possessed by the devil," they fought Vodoun in a more or less coherent fashion.

To achieve victory, however, the clergy needed sustained and wholehearted backing from the government and the collaboration of the learned class. But the authorities could not risk their slim popular support by attacking Vodoun openly; nor were they willing to risk giving a foreign clergy the means to gain much control over the masses. Since political instability made tenure in office precarious and short, there was a sore lack of continuity in policy. Furthermore, a new president was more apt to adopt an attitude towards Vodoun that was opposite to that of his predecessor. Finally, politicians in general (including members of the educated class) were either dependent upon Vodoun for support or in debt to it. The anti-Vodoun leagues, the pastoral letters, the local successes of individual priests consequently amounted to little.

During the American Occupation, official hostility to Vodoun could not be fully exploited by the Catholic clergy. The central issue for the Haitian was nationalism, but for the French priests the matter of cultural and religious influences was also at stake. The Occupation carried in its wake the danger of Protestantism and the adoption of new customs. The clergy preferred to side with the bourgeoisie which was chaffing at the presence of a dominant foreign group, the Americans. It was not until 1941, under the presidency of Lescot, that Catholicism, for the first time in Haitian history, had a free hand to deal with Vodoun under ideal conditions, i.e., total collaboration with the government. At that time, "the anti-superstitious campaign" was launched, and its methods reached a high pitch of intolerance. Vodoun temples were sacked, the paraphernalia were burned and the believers were forced to "renounce" their faith.

The campaign took place, however, at the very moment when the war effort of the United States had required and obtained from the Haitian Government the means of starting a rubber production program. Peasant lands were expropriated and thoughtless destruction of fruit trees and cultivated plots took place. Faced with the menace of general discontent, the authorities had to stop the inquisitorial activities of the clergy. Thus the government which had given its blessing to the campaign had to come to the defense of Vodoun. In February 1942, shots fired in the Catholic chapel of Delmas during the Sunday Mass served notice to Catholicism that it had failed in its enterprise. The mistake of the Lescot government partly contributed to its downfall in 1946. Thereafter Vodoun was not molested officially.

Protestantism had begun to penetrate Haiti as early as 1830. Later, the immigration of Negroes from the United States who were invited by Haiti to help develop cotton plantations, gave Protestantism a broader foothold in the country. Its spread, even during the years of Occupation, was modest. But Protestantism holds a ponderous asset: it is not associated with Vodoun. It has remained immune to the syncretizing which had blended African and Catholic rituals from the beginning of the French rule of Haiti. The Vodounist believes in the Christian God as an almighty separate Being, but the saints have become closely associated with the *loas* or African spirits whenever their attributes, as they appear in images and sculptures, correspond to the age, functions, or symbols of their Vodoun counterparts.[18] Consequently, the believer who has failed in his obligation towards the spirits can expect little protection from Catholicism for these same spirits may be present in the place of worship. No line can be drawn in this respect.

Protestantism, however, uses no images. In its temples the fleeing Vodounist feels safer.[19] Protestantism is also much more strict about the behavior of its converts than Catholicism is. It admits no compromise with or tolerance of Vodoun. As a result the Protestant peasant develops a singular hatred for anything folkloric, such as tales, dancing, and drumming. He spends his free time singing hymns. The mechanical concept of refuge or protection explains some of the appeal of the numerous Protestant denominations for a limited sector of the Haitian peasantry, but we can go further. Escape from costly ceremonies to the *loas* and hope of actually recovering from illnesses might well move the bulk of converts, as Métraux explains.[20] Yet, another socio-cultural factor at work is non-conformism, *the reaction of Vodounists to Vodoun.* The ideas spread by agronomists, physicians, priests, ministers and the like about the possibility of a better life have found an echo among the more ambitious and progressive elements of the peasantry, few as they may be. They are ready to try fertilizers, contour cultivation, irrigation, new crops, and to learn to read and write. In a word, they want to break away from tradition, a tradition whose axis is Vodoun.

We do not mean to imply that Protestantism is the salvation of Haiti, nor the solution for its ailments. We have known Catholic ruralites who were as eager to follow the path of change in both religious and secular matters; who gave up polygamy as an uneconomical practice and laughed at Vodoun. By 1957, the cooperative moyement which might have made decisive changes in Haiti, was beginning to bud in the countryside. The peasantry needed only a sustained official program of technical assistance to start moving steadily away from routine and the supernatural. Instead they got Duvalier. Instead of receiving agricultural guidance, schools, and clinics, they suffered the extortions of the militia and an overdose of Vodoun to kill their pains or to keep them in awe. Vodoun, which at times had been an instrument of union, became a tool of coercion, the whip of internal colonialism, a means for the exploitation of the Black by the Black. Such are the fruits of its triumph.

The *zombi,* the legendary soulless robot, once made Haiti infamous. Duvalier has *zombified* his country. According to folklore, the *zombi* must be fed salt in order to regain his faculties. When Duvalier goes, who will feed salt, the salt of life to a whole nation? In other words, what is the future of Haiti? We can only surmise that the recovery will be long and painful. Surely there will be a reaction against Vodoun. It has been discredited by being too closely associated with a destructive regime. Perhaps both Catholic and Protestant clergies will be chastened by their ordeal and with a newly gained cohesion they will set themselves resolutely to the task of providing the masses with material and spiritual help. May the *clercs,* cured of folklore at long last, learn the lesson from the progressive peasant and choose to lead the van.

FOOTNOTES

1. Philip D. Curtin, *Two Jamaicas,* Cambridge: Harvard University Press, 1955, p. 36.
2. Métraux, 1958, p. 298. [pp. 335-336 in Charteris' translation. — Ed.]
3. C. Lévi-Strauss, *Tristes tropiques,* Paris: Librairie Plon, 1955, 462 pp.
4. J. S. Slotkin, *Social Anthropology,* New York: The Macmillan Company, 1950, pp. 182 ff.
5. Jahn, 1961, p. 54.
6. A *houngan* is an initiate, a priest. The *bocor* is a magician or medicine man. *Houngans* do cure and practice magic, but no *bocor* officiates at Vodoun ceremonies. The word *bocor* has a sinister ring about it.
7. Mennesson-Rigaud, 1953, p. 236.
8. The Vodoun pantheon increases with the passing of time and events. The United States Marine Corps left a *loa* in Haiti; when he possesses a believer (a trance-like state) he asks, with an unmistakably American accent, for corned beef and whiskey, a rather expensive taste.
9. The former Spanish colony voluntarily joined Haiti in 1820, becoming independent 24 years later. The unification of the island, a dream of L'Ouverture and Dessalines, was thus shattered.
10. Rigaud, 1953.
11. Lescot further distinguished himself by approving the anti-Vodoun campaign undertaken by the Catholic Church in 1941. See p. 65.
12. Robert H. Lowie, *Social Organization,* New York: Rinehart and Company, 1948, p. 317.
13. Duvalier's task was made easier by the ten months of political troubles which followed General Magloire's fall. As early as June 1957, the

Chief of Staff, Antonio T. Kébrau, had purged the army of numerous privates and NCO's suspected of loyalty to Provisional President Daniel Fignolé whom he had overthrown.

14. Robert Debbs Heinl, Jr., "Terror in Haiti: A Case Study in Freedom," *The New Republic,* May 16, 1964, p. 19.

15. Dessalines, the Liberator of Haiti and its first Emperor, is best remembered by the common folk for his hatred of the "whites" — the French. Duvalier frequently compares his task with that which confronted the Emperor in 1803. His followers do not hesitate to put both men on the same level of greatness.

16. In his notebooks written during World War II and published posthumously, Lévy-Bruhl reneged on the theory of "Primitive mentality" to which he owed his celebrity.

17. Alfred Rosenberg, champion of the *Deutsche Glaubensbewegung,* was admiringly quoted by François Duvalier and the late Lorimer Denis, 1944, p. 32.

18. Michel Leiris, "Note sur l'usage des chromolithographies catholiques par les vodouisants d'Haïti," in *Les Afro-Américains, Mémoires de l'Institut Français d'Afrique Noire,* Dakar, 1953, pp. 201-207.

19. However, the Episcopalian cathedral of Port-au-Prince has been decorated by Haitian popular painters with a series of "frescoes" depicting scenes of the New Testament.

20. Métraux, 1958, pp. 311 ff. [pp. 351 ff. in Charteris' translation. — Ed.]

ANNOTATED BIBLIOGRAPHY

Selected and Annotated by Rémy Bastien

ALAUX, Gustave d'
1858   *L'Empereur Soulouque et son empire.* Paris: Lévy.

French irony and mischief at their best. Contains frequent references to Vodoun and its role in the politics of the Empire. When one chooses to ignore the qualities of Soulouque as a statesman, he becomes a grotesque and easy target.

BASTIEN, Rémy
1951   *La Familia rural haitiana: Valle de Marbial.* Mexico: Libra. 184 pp.

Studies the decadence of family life and economy of the valley of Marbial in 1948. Vodoun had been almost eradicated seven years before and had not recovered from the blow. Protestants are shown as an active and economically progressive minority.

BELLEGARDE, Dantès
1953   *Histoire du peuple haïtien, 1492-1952.* Port-au-Prince. 365 pp.

A mulatto and member of the bourgeoisie, Bellegarde has been criticized for his extreme position in favor of the "French character of Haitian culture." However, his patriotism and honesty have compelled respect from all, friends and foes.

BONSAL, Stephen
1912   *The American Mediterranean.* New York: Moffat, Yard and Co. 488 pp.

Contemporary with Teddy Roosevelt's "Big Stick" policy, this suave diplomat devotes some interesting pages to Haiti and the control exercised by Vodoun upon President Antoine Simon.

CABON, Rév. Adolphe
1933   *Notes sur l'histoire religieuse d'Haïti de la révolution au concordat (1789-1860).* Port-au-Prince: Petit Séminaire, Collège St. Martial. 520 pp.

A sober narrative of the diplomatic activities which led to the Concordat of 1860. Cabon also wrote an excellent factual *History of Haiti.* The French priest devoted the best of his life to the country; his equanimity is blameless.

CHAZOTTE, Pierre Étienne
        See Platt.

COURLANDER, Harold
1939   *Haiti Singing*. Chapel Hill: University of North Carolina Press. 273 pp.

1960   *The Drum and the Hoe: Life and Lore of the Haitian People*. Berkeley and Los Angeles: University of California Press. 371 pp.

Courlander did for the music of Haiti what Leyburn did for its sociology and Herskovits for its rural life.

CRAIGE, John H.
1933   *Black Bagdad*. New York: Minton, Balch & Co. 276 pp.

One of the too many superficial books on Haiti.

DAVIS, H. P.
1928   *Black Democracy: The Story of Haiti*. New York: L. MacVeagh, The Dial Press. 370 pp.

The author who knew Haiti first hand and started castor oil production during World War I, although sympathetic, shows little comprehension of the political problems of the country. Incidental references to Vodoun.

DENIS, Lorimer and François DUVALIER
1944   "L'Évolution stadiale du vodou." *Bulletin du Bureau d'Ethnologie d'Haïti*, 3, 9-32. Port-au-Prince.

This text of a lecture delivered at the City Hall of Port-au-Prince by the late Lorimer Denis in January 1944 sustains the thesis that the Independence of Haiti was the fruit of Vodoun. The hostility of Toussaint L'Ouverture and Dessalines to the cult is conveniently ignored.

DEREN, Maya
1953   *Divine Horsemen: The Living Gods of Haiti*. London and New York: Thames and Hudson. 350 pp.

After World War II, Vodoun attracted a large number of passionate apologists. This book, good when treating of music and dancing, becomes annoying when dealing in a pseudo-scientific fashion with the meaning of Vodoun.

DUVALIER, François
        See Denis.

FRANKLIN, James
1828   *The Present State of Hayti (Santo Domingo), with Remarks on Its Agriculture, Commerce, Laws, Religion, Finances and Population . . . .* London: J. Murray. 411 pp.

At the time of Franklin's visit, the whole island of Hispaniola made up the Republic of Hayti as it was officially spelled. Franklin is one of many British travelers, business-men, and ministers who paid attention to the country with a possible view to develop commerce with England or to plan missionary work. The best known are the Rev. S. W. Hanna, John Candler, Charles Mackensie, the Rev. Mark B. Bird. They are usually sympathetic to Haiti, and provide most useful data about the peasant's life and beliefs.

HERSKOVITS, Melville J.
1937 *Life in a Haitian Valley*. New York: Knopf. 350 pp.

At long last a professional American anthropologist came . . . .

HURSTON, Zora Neal
1939 *Voodoo Gods: An Inquiry into Native Myths and Magic in Jamaica and Haiti*. London: J. M. Dent & Sons. 290 pp.

Typical of the genre "I came, I saw, I wrote." Journalistic and often pretentious.

JAHN, Janheinz
1961 *Muntu: An Outline of the New African Culture*. Translated by Marjorie Grene. New York: Grove Press, Inc. 267 pp.

A sample of the enthusiasm for the discovery of African and Afro-American cultures. Chapter II, "Voodoo," sets the religion of Haiti within the metaphysics of African philosophy.

LÉGER, Jacques-Nicolas
1907 *Haïti: Son histoire et ses détracteurs*. New York and Washington: The Neale Publishing Company. 372 pp. [An English translation entitled *Haiti: Her History and Her Detractors* was published simultaneously by the same company. — Ed.]

A distinguished diplomat and statesman, the author wrote a brave defense of Haiti at a difficult time in its history. His tendency is to minimize the importance of Vodoun.

LEYBURN, James G.
1945 *The Haitian People*. New Haven: Yale University Press. 342 pp.

Scholarly, objective, and understanding, Leyburn wrote a classic. Haiti's blind political troubles were given a sound socio-economic interpretation. Vodoun is but an inci-dental topic.

LOEDERER, Richard A.
1935 *Voodoo Fire in Haiti*. New York: Doubleday, Doran & Co., Inc. 274 pp.

Poor followers of Seabrook are not lacking in the literature of Vodoun.

MARCELIN, Pierre
    See Thoby-Marcelin.

MÉTRAUX, Alfred
1958   *Le Vaudou haïtien*. Paris: Gallimard. [Published in English as *Voodoo in Haiti*. Trans-
    lated by Hugo Charteris. New York: Oxford University Press. 400 pp.]

    A veteran ethnographer, Métraux offers some good interpretations of the social struc-
    ture of Vodoun, its magic, and its resistance to Catholicism.

MORAL, Paul
1961   *Le Paysan haïtien*. Paris: Maisonneuve et Larose. 375 pp.

    Vodoun is hardly mentioned in this important work whose concern is with the forma-
    tion of the peasantry, its economic activities and prospective capacity to change.

NILES, Blair
1926   *Black Hayti: A Biography of Africa's Eldest Daughter*. New York: G. P. Putnam's Sons.
    325 pp.

    Scores of books of average and below average quality appeared during the twenties.
    They normally put emphasis on the political instability of the country and the dark
    aspects of Vodoun.

PETERS, Rev. Carl E.
1941   *Lumière sur le humfort*. Port-au-Prince: Chéraquit. 55 pp.

    Written by a Catholic priest born in Haiti of foreign parents, it is a violent and often
    passionate attack on Vodoun. The date of publication coincides with the "anti-super-
    stitious campaign" launched with the backing of the government.

PLATT, Charles, Ed.
1927   *The Black Rebellion in Haiti*. By Pierre Étienne Chazotte. Philadelphia: Privately
    printed. 122 pp.

    The original was written in 1804 by a former French planter, Chazotte, who became an
    American citizen and as such was not molested during the massacre ordered by Des-
    salines in 1804. The report was first published in New York in 1840 and only one copy
    seems to exist in the Library of Congress. The privately printed edition of 1927 is only
    half the original one. It contains hardly a good word about the Haitian leaders. For that
    reason, perhaps, it was thought convenient to publish it during the American
    Occupation.

PRICE-MARS, Jean
1928   *Ainsi parla l'oncle. . . : Essais d'ethnographie*. Paris: Imprimerie de Compiègne. 243 pp.

    Price-Mars founded the Haitian school of ethnology. Part of this famous book is an open and objective defense of Vodoun, the first of its kind. The remaining chapters form a rather poor ethnographic picture of peasant life.

RIGAUD, Milo

1953   *La Tradition voudoo et le voudoo häitien.* Paris: Niclaus. 433 pp.

Poet, painter, and novelist, Milo Rigaud knows his Vodoun well, but his book is strictly esoteric, with, at times, some unfounded philological deductions and historical interpretations.

ROUMAIN, Jacques

1944   *Gouverneurs de la rosée.* Port-au-Prince: Imprimerie de l'État. 321 pp. [Published under title *Masters of the Dew* by Hitchcock, N. Y., in the translation of Langston Hughes.]

Poet, novelist, and anthropologist, Roumain, a Marxist, fought against the "campaign" of the Catholic clergy. His novel and last work, *Masters of the Dew*, exploits the *couleur locale* of Vodoun without exalting the religion.

ST.-JOHN, Spenser

1884   *Hayti, or the Black Republic.* London: Smith, Elder & Co. 334 pp.

The British Seabrook of the late nineteenth century, but with a bitterness and false self-righteousness entirely lacking in the American. Made Haiti infamous as a land of anthropophagists.

SEABROOK, William B.

1929   *The Magic Island.* New York: Harcourt, Brace & Co. 336 pp.

Behind Seabrook's mythomania and sensationalism, one can feel his liking for Haiti and its people. Epoch-making, *Magic Island* associated sex and blood with Vodoun.

THOBY-MARCELIN, Philippe and Pierre MARCELIN

1944   *Canapé-vert.* New York: Éditions de la Maison Française, Inc. 255 pp.

This novel was followed by *The Pencil of God.* Both treat of Haitian rural or urban life and are exceptional in that they show the disintegrating effects of Vodoun and magic upon individuals and community. Compare them with Jacques S. Alexis' *Les Arbres musiciens,* where Vodoun, shown as felicific, is opposed to magic. However, Alexis believes that technology will eventually dispose of Vodoun.

VERSCHUEREN, Rév. J. (Pseudonym)

1948   *La République d'Haïti.* Wetteren: Éd. Scaldis et Paris. 3 Vols.

In spite of its impressive size this work of a Belgian priest contains little novelty. Its passages on Vodoun are obviously biased and over credulous.

SUPPLEMENTARY BIBLIOGRAPHY

The following citations were compiled primarily from the card catalog of the Library of Congress. ICR will present a more comprehensive bibliography in a future publication.

ANONYMOUS
[1961?] *Études, démographiques, économiques, et sociologiques.* Series 1, 2, and 3. Port-au-Prince: Département de la Santé Publique et de la Population.

ANONYMOUS
1954 "The Whistle and the Whip." *Tomorrow* 3 (1), 91-94.

BASCOM, William R.
1952 "Two Forms of Afro-Cuban Divination." In Sol Tax, Ed., *Acculturation in the Americas.* Chicago: University of Chicago Press. 169-179.

BASTIEN, Rémy
1947 "The Negro in Haiti." In *The Negro Yearbook.* Alabama: Tuskeegee Institute. 617-631.

1951 "Haiti: ayer y hoy." *Cuadernos Americanos* 10 (3), 153-163. Mexico City.

1952 "El vodu en Haiti." Reprinted from *Cuadernos Americanos.* Mexico City. 24 pp.

BELLEGARDE, Dantès
1938 *La nation haïtienne.* Paris: J. de Gigord. 361 pp.

1953 *Haïti et son peuple.* Paris: Nouvelles Éditions Latines. 121 pp.

[n.d.] *Haïti et ses problèmes.* Montreal: Bernard Valiquette. 297 pp.

BIJOU, L.
    See Wittkower, E. D.

BONHOMME, Colbert
1957 *Révolution et contra-révolution en Haïti de 1946 à 1957.* Port-au-Prince: Imprimerie de l'État.

BOURGUIGNON, Erika
1959 "The Persistence of Folk Belief: Some Notes on Cannibalism and Zombis in Haiti." *American Journal of Folklore* 72 (283), 36-46.

BOURGUIGNON, Erika and Louanna PETTAY
1963   "Spirit Possession, Trance, and Cross-Cultural Research." Annual Spring Meeting, American Ethnological Society. Mimeo. 20 pp. (Appears also in *Proceedings*, Symposium on Community Studies in Anthropology, Annual Spring Meeting, American Ethnological Society, 1963. Seattle, Washington, 1964. 36-46.)

BOWMAN, Laura
1938   *The Voice of Haiti: Original Ceremonial Songs, Voodoo Chants, Drum Beats*. New York: Clarence Williams Music Publishing Co.

CANNOŃ, W. B.
1942   "Voodoo Death." *American Anthropologist* 44 (2), 169-181.

CASIMIR, Jean
1964   "Aperçu sur la structure économique d'Haïti." *América Latina* 7 (3), 37-56. Rio de Janeiro.

CHACÓN Y CALVO, José María, et al.
1955   *Miscelánea de estudios dedicados a Fernando Ortíz por sus discípulos, colegas, y amigos*. 3 Vols. Habana: [pub. unknown]. 1621 pp.

CHRISTOPHONTE, P.
1950   *Deuxième thèse de doctorat*. Port-au-Prince: Imprimerie Beaubrun.

CLOUZOT, H. G.
1951   *Le cheval des dieux*. Paris: Julliard.

COMHAIRE-SYLVAIN, Suzanne
1938   *A propos du vocabulaire des croyances paysannes*. Port-au-Prince: [pub. unknown]. 12 pp.

COOK, M., Ed.
1951   *Haiti*. Washington, D. C.: Pan American Union.

COURLANDER, Harold
1941   "Haiti's Political Folksongs." *Opportunity* 19 (4), 114-118.

1944   "Gods of the Haitian Mountains." *Journal of Negro History* 29 (3), 339-372.

1954   "Gods of Haiti." *Tomorrow* 3 (1), 53-60.

1955   "The Loa of Haiti: New World African Deities." In *Miscelánea de estudios dedicados* a *Fernando Ortíz por sus discipulos, colegas, y amigos,* Vol. 1. Habana: [pub. un-known]. 142-443.

DAUMEC, Lucien
1954   *La mission des élites.* Port-au-Prince: Imprimerie "Les Presses Libres." 35 pp.

DENIS, Lorimer
        See Duvalier, F.

1963   "Médecine populaire." *Bulletin du Bureau d'Ethnologie d'Haïti* 4 (29), 37-39.
        Port-au-Prince.

DENIS, Lorimer and François DUVALIER
1948   *Le problème des classes à travers l'histoire d'Haïti.* [Publisher and place of publication
        not cited]. 128 pp.

DEROSE, Rodolphe
1956   *Caractère culture vodou: Formation et interpretation de l'individualité haïtienne.*
        Port-au-Prince: Bibliothèque Haïtienne. 240 pp.

DE YOUNG, Maurice
1958   *Man and Land in the Haitian Economy.* Gainesville: University of Florida Press, Latin
        American Monographs, No. 3.

DORSAINVIL, Justin Chrysostome
1937   *Psychologie haïtienne: Vodou et magie.* Port-au-Prince: Imprimerie Nemours
        Télhomme.

1952   *Essais de vulgarisation scientifique et questions haïtiennes.* Port-au-Prince: Imprimerie
        Théodore. 166 pp.

DOUYON, Emerson
        See Wittkower, E. D.

1965   "La crise de possession dans le vaudou haïtien." Ph.D. Thesis, University of Montreal.
        303 pp.

DUVALIER, François and Lorimer DENIS
        See also Denis, L.

1936   "Les civilisations de l'Afrique noire et le problème haïtien." *Revue de la Société
        Haïtienne d'Histoire et de Géographie* 7 (23), 1-29. Port-au-Prince.

DUVIVIER, Ulrick
1941   *Bibliographie générale et méthodique d'Haïti*. 2 Vols. Port-au-Prince: Imprimerie de l'État.

ERASMUS, Charles J.
1952   "Agricultural Changes in Haiti: Patterns of Resistance and Acceptance." *Human Organization* 11, 25-26.

GEORGES-JACOB, Kléber
1941   *L'Ethnie haïtienne*. Port-au-Prince: Imprimerie de l'État.

HALL, Robert A., Jr.
1953   "Haitian Creole: Grammar, Texts, Vocabulary." *American Anthropologist* 55 (No. 2, part 2), Memoir No. 74, 309 pp.

HALL, Robert B.
1929   "The Société Congo of the Ile à Gonave." *American Anthropologist* 31, 685-700.

HYPPOLITE, Michelson Paul
1952   "Le devenir du créole haïtien." Conférence prononcée au pavillon des beaux-arts le 7 août 1952. Port-au-Prince: Imprimerie de l'État. 23 pp.

1954   *A Study of Haitian Folklore*. [Translated by Edgar Laforest and Pansy Hart.] Port-au-Prince: Imprimerie de l'État. 51 pp.

KIEV, Ari
1961   "Folk Psychiatry in Haiti." *Journal of Nervous and Mental Disorders* 132, 260-265.

1961   "Spirit Possession in Haiti." *American Journal of Psychiatry* 118, 133-141.

1962   "The Psychotherapeutic Aspects of Primitive Medicine." *Human Organization* 21, 25-29.

KREHM, William
1960   *Democracias y tiranías en el Caribe*. [Habana?]: Editora Popular de Cuba y de Caribe.

LOBB, John
1940   "Caste and Class in Haiti." *American Journal of Sociology* 46, 23-34.

LUBIN, Maurice A.
1952   "Productions intellectuelles haïtiennes de 1942 à 1952." Typed manuscript. 30 pp.

MANIGAT, Leslie François
1964   *Haiti of the Sixties, Object of International Concern.* Washington, D. C.: Washington
        Center of Foreign Policy Research. 104 pp.

MARCELIN, Milo
1949   *Mythologie vodou.* 3 Vols. Port-au-Prince: Les Éditions Haïtiennes.

MARS, Louis
1938   "Délire mystique à thème vaudouique." *Les Griots: Revue Scientifique et Littéraire
        d'Haiti* 2 (2), 281-285. Port-au-Prince.

1946   *La crise de possession dans le vaudou: Essais de psychiatrie comparée.* Port-au-Prince:
        Bibliothèque de l'Institut d'Ethnologie. 103 pp.

1963   "Nouvelle contribution à l'étude de la crise de possession." *Ethnologie: Congrès Inter-
        national des Sciences Anthropologiques et Ethnologiques,* VI, 1960. Paris: Musée de
        l'Homme. 543-544.

MAXIMILIEN, Louis
[1945?] *Le vodou haïtien: Rite radas—canzo.* Port-au-Prince: Imprimerie de l'État. 224 pp.

MENNESSON-RIGAUD, Odette
1952   "Étude sur le culte des marassas en Haïti." *Zaïre* 6 (6), 597-621. Louvain.

1953   "Vodou haitien: Quelques notes sur ses réminiscences africaines." In *Les Afro-Améri-
        cains: Mémoires de l'Institut Français d'Afrique Noire,* No. 27, 235-238. Dakar.

MÉTRAUX, Alfred
1954   "Divinités et cultes vodou dans la vallée de Marbial (Haïti)." *Zaïre* 8 (7), 675-707.
        Louvain.

1960   *Haiti: Black Peasants and Voodoo.* New York: Universe Books.

MÉTRAUX, Rhoda
1951   "Kith and Kin: A Study of Creole Social Structure in Marbial, Haiti." Microfilm. Ann
        Arbor: University Microfilms.

MORAL, Paul
1959   *L'économie haïtienne.* Port-au-Prince: Imprimerie de l'État. 190 pp.

PAUL, Emmanuel Casseus
1946   *Notes sur le folklore d'Haïti: Proverbes et chansons.* Port-au-Prince: Imprimerie
        Télhomme. 80 pp.

1949   L'Ethnographie en Haïti: Ses initiateurs, son état actuel, ses tâches et son avenir. Port-au-Prince: Imprimerie de l'État. 40 pp.

1962   Panorama du folklore haïtien: Présence africaine en Haïti. Port-au-Prince: Imprimerie de l'État.

PETTAY, Louanna
    See Bourguignon, Erika

PHAREAUX, Lallier C.
1953   La vie contemporaine: Collection du tricinquantenaire de l'indépendance d'Haïti. Port-au-Prince: Imprimerie de l'État. 630 pp.

PRICE-MARS, Jean
1939   Formation ethnique folk-lore et culture du peuple haïtien. Port-au-Prince: V. Valgin.

1945   "Culte des marassas." Afroamericana 1 (1, 2), 41-49. Mexico City.

1948   "Sociologie religieuse: La République d'Haïti." Revue de la Société Haïtienne d'Histoire et de Géographie 19 (71), 1-21. Port-au-Prince.

1951   "Folklore et patriotisme." Conférence prononcée sous les auspices de l'alliance française le novembre 1951. Port-au-Prince: Imprimerie "Les Presses Libres." 22 pp.

1953   "Folklore et patriotisme." Revue de la Société Haïtienne d'Histoire et de Géographie 23 (84), 1-16. Port-au-Prince.

1953   La République d'Haïti et la République Dominicaine: Les aspects divers d'un problème d'histoire, de géographie et d'ethnologie. 2 Vols. Port-au-Prince: [pub. unknown].

1959   De Saint-Domingue à Haïti: Essai sur la culture, les arts et la littérature. Paris: Présence Africaine. 170 pp.

1960   Silhouettes des nègres et de négrophiles. Paris: Présence Africaine.

[n.d.]   Un étape de l'évolution haïtienne. Port-au-Prince: Imprimerie "La Presse." 208 pp.

RODMAN, Selden
1954   Haiti: The Black Republic. New York: Devin-Adair Company. 168 pp.

RODRIGUEZ, Manuel Tomás
1962   Papá Legbá (La crónica del voudú o pacto con el diablo). Santo Domingo: [pub. unknown]. 2nd edition. 195 pp. (1st edition printed in 1945, Ciudad Trujillo: Imprimerie Arte y Cine).

ROMAIN, J. B.
1963 "L'homme haïtien: Ses origines ethniques, sa psychologie." *Ethnologie: Congrès International des Sciences Anthropologiques et Ethnologiques*, VI, 1960. Paris: Musée de l'Homme. 243-246.

RONCÉRAY, Hubert de
1961 "Crise de la transition de la société haïtienne." *Revue de la Faculté d'Ethnologie* 4, 31-39. Port-au-Prince.

SAINT SURIN, Jacques
1962 *Indices démographiques et perspectives de la population d'Haïti de 1950 à 1980.* Port-au-Prince: Imprimerie de l'État. 36 pp.

SCHAEDEL, Richard P.
1962 "An Essay on the Human Resources of Haiti." (Mimeographed) United States Agency for International Development: USAID/Haiti. 117 pp.

SIMPSON, George E.
1940 "Haitian Peasant Economy." *Journal of Negro History* 25 (4), 498-519.

STERLIN, Philippe
1954 *Vèvès vodou.* Série II. Port-au-Prince: Éditions Philippe Sterlin. 48 pp.

STREET, John M.
1960 *Historical and Economic Geography of the Southwestern Peninsula of Haiti.* Berkeley: Department of Geography, University of California.

STYCOS, J. Mayone
1964 "Haitian Attitudes Toward Family Size." *Human Organization* 23 (1), 42-47.

SYLVAIN, Jeanne G.
1949 "La infancia campesina en el valle de Marbial (Haiti)." *America Indígena* 9 (4), 299-332. Mexico City.

VERGER, Pierre
1957 "Notes sur le culte des orisa et vodun à Bahia, la baie de tous les saints, au Brésil et à l'ancienne côte des esclaves en Afrique." *Mémoires de l'Institut Français d'Afrique Noire*, No. 51. Dakar. 609 pp.

VIAU, Alfred
1955 *Negros, mulatos, blancos.* Ciudad Trujillo: Editora Montalvo. 223 pp.

WILLIAMS, Samuel H.
1949   *Voodoo Roads*. Wien: Verlag Für Jugend und Volk. 111 pp.

WINGFIELD, Roland and Vernon J. PARENTON
1965   "Class Structure and Class Conflict in Haitian Society." *Social Forces* 43(3), 338-347.

WITTKOWER, E. D., L. DOUYON, and L. BIJOU
1964   "Spirit Possession in Haitian Vodun Ceremonies." *Acta Psychotherapeutica et Psycho-somatica* 12, 72-80. Basel.

WOOD, Harold A.
1963   *Northern Haiti: Land, Land Use, and Settlement: A Geographical Investigation of the Département du Nord*. Toronto: University of Toronto Press.

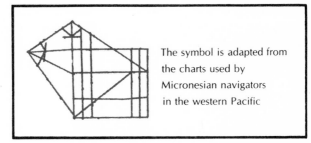

The symbol is adapted from
the charts used by
Micronesian navigators
in the western Pacific

The type face used in this book is 10 point Optima
with a 2 point leading and was set by General Typographers,
Inc., of Washington, D. C. It was printed by the offset lithograph process
on Mead Suede Book Substance 70.

E. Smith Associates, Washington, D. C., designed the book and prepared it for printing.